PREPARING

FOR

EASTER

**Newly revised and enlarged
according to the spirit and directives
of the Restored Holy Week Services**

By Reverend Clifford Howell, S.J.

THE LITURGICAL PRESS

ST. JOHN'S ABBEY • COLLEGEVILLE, MINNESOTA

PREPARING FOR EASTER is but one item in a series of publications on the liturgy and related topics, e.g., Holy Mass, Sacraments, Liturgical Year, Church Music, Sacramentals, Sacred Pictures. Descriptive catalogs will be sent gratis upon request. Address: The Liturgical Press, Collegeville, Minnesota.

Imprimi postest: Daniel H. Conway, S.J., Provincial of the Missouri Province. *Imprimi potest:* ✠ Baldwin Dworschak, O.S.B., D.D., Abbot of St. John's Abbey. *Nihil obstat:* John Eidenschink, O.B.S., *Censor deputatus. Imprimatur:* ✠ Peter W. Bartholome, D.D., Bishop of St. Cloud. January 6, 1957.

CONTENTS

FOREWORD

This book has been written for the purpose of fostering appreciation for the great liturgical treasure which we have received from His Holiness Pope Pius XII in the form of the Restored Order of Holy Week, and of enabling both clergy and laity to take part in all its rites with more profit through a deepened understanding of their content and implications.

The restoration was begun by the decree of February 9th, 1951, concerning the Easter Vigil. In this decree the Sacred Congregation of Rites says that "the Church, from the earliest ages, used to celebrate the Vigil with the utmost solemnity . . . during the hours of the night that precedes the Resurrection of our Lord. In the course of time, however, its celebration was, for a variety of reasons, transposed to the morning hours of Holy Saturday . . . but not without detriment to its original symbolism."

The restoration of the Vigil to its former hour and the revision of its text were dictated by no mere concern for archeology; the predominant motive has been pastoral; what is sought is primarily the good of souls.

The way to attain this object is, then, to eliminate the "detriment to the original symbolism"—that is, to make the symbolism, now revised and restored, do very thoroughly what it is designed to do. It is meant to *signify* to the people the great spiritual reality which underlies the whole rite. What is required, then, is the maximum of understanding by the people of what it is all about.

In practically every church where the restored Vigil has been carried out, its reception has been enthusiastic. But this fact alone is no proof that it has been truly effective of its *intrinsic* purpose. It may well be that the people have been delighted with its novelty, with its picturesqueness, with the thrill of having something interesting to watch and to do, with the impressiveness of the gradual spread of the candle flames in the darkened church.

They have been captivated indeed; but perhaps, as yet, only with the externals. Unless these externals are thoroughly understood in their meaning—unless, in fact, they become genuine significative symbols rather than interesting and beautiful sights—the Vigil will not produce those spiritual effects which are inherent in it. As the years go by and the novelty wears off, the appeal of the mere externals will grow less.

It is imperative, therefore, that the appreciation which the faithful now have of this ceremony should be deepened; they must be helped to penetrate through these externals, and to achieve that renewal of mind and heart and will which alone constitutes the genuine good of their souls.

Exactly the same may be said of all the other Holy Week Ceremonies, reformed and restored by the decree *Maxima Redemptionis* of November 16, 1955. That, doubtless, is why the *Instructio* which follows it repeats, even more emphatically, the directive given in 1951 concerning the need for preparation. "Local Ordinaries," it says, "are carefully to ensure that priests, especially those entrusted with the care of souls, are well instructed not only concerning the ritual celebration of the restored *Ordo* of Holy Week, but also concerning its liturgical meaning and pastoral purpose. Besides this they are to make sure that the faithful also are given, during the course of Lent, instructions that will enable them properly to understand the restored *Ordo,* so that they may devoutly take part in its celebration both with mind and heart" (*Instructio* I.n.1).

From this we may deduce that any priest who carries out the rite, however perfectly as regards its ceremonial, without such preparatory instruction of his people, will fail to do for their souls that which is really the aim and object of the whole celebration. What is required for them is a true spiritual resurrection, a vivid re-incorporation into Christ by their paschal Communion, a determined grip on their baptismal obligations, a new and profound adhesion to Christ their Savior and their Head, a fresh dedication to a holy Christian life.

This must not be a mere arousing of emotions, just some sort of pious thrill passing in its effects. Nor is it to be just an affair of morals. It is to be something actually effected in their souls. This it is which ought to be the result of their participation in Holy Week; the rites are to be the external sign of this inward reality—they are meant to be *sacramental.*

This is precisely what we are told by the *Decretum* itself; the liturgical ceremonies of Holy Week "have not only a singular dignity, but are endowed with a sacramental efficacy and power to nourish the Christian life." Obviously this does not mean that they produce their effects *ex opere operato,* as do the seven sacraments; the power which is latent in them requires the co-operation of those who are to obtain their benefits.

The rites, however beautiful, can never produce such a deep effect on people who do not appreciate their full significance. That is why it is so important that people be instructed beforehand. They must be helped to discover, within the rites and texts, the salvific effects—the divine action—which is at work in the celebration of the paschal Mysteries. To these they must open their minds and hearts; to these they must respond with their wills from the very depths of their being.

That means that they must see the vast perspective of the paschal Mysteries as a whole. They have to grasp them, as the application here and now to their own souls, of the whole economy of salvation as wrought in the first instance historically by Christ our Lord, and carried on now mystically by the same Christ active in and through His Mystical Body, the Church.

The salvation of mankind was effected initially in the historical order. Which means that the whole of the liturgy is set in a historical framework. The entire story, from the Fall to the Parousia, the Second Coming, must be laid before them as an intelligible whole. They cannot understand the paschal mysteries properly unless they are given some grasp of all this as a unity, even though details of the picture be lacking.

It is the story of God's dealings with man from beginning to end. What He effected partially by signs and types in the Old Testament He wrought more fully and perfectly by the historic actions of Christ in the New Testament. He carries on the work now on a new plane—that of sacramental signs. Finally He will bring it to its conclusion with the end of the world, at the Second Coming of Christ, when all these signs will give way to the thing signified.

In other words, the future is involved, as well as the past. To explain to people the historical background is not enough; they must also have the eschatological outlook if the balance is to be right. This is so because the present order of sacramental signs does but prefigure and promise in its turn the full realization of God's plan for the salvation of mankind; and this is not complete until the "Day of the Lord" which shall bring the "resurrection of the body and life everlasting."

We conclude, therefore, that the preparation of the people for Holy Week *must* be of the nature of a *biblical* cate-chesis. The texts and gestures and things used in the rites are saturated with biblical images, symbols and allusions. Fire, light, wax, oil, incense, must all be pregnant with meaning for the people; Noe, Abraham, Isaac, Melchisedech, Moses and all the others must not be mere names; the ark, the Red Sea, the pillar of fire, the manna, the paschal lamb must not be mere things. All must have their wondrous connotations, must evoke stirring memories, bring up vivid pictures in the minds of the faithful who see and hear.

They must feel that they themselves are part of this amazing story, actors in it here and now because it is not yet finished. They belong in this history, are making this history, just as truly as did the Israelites who fled from Pharao, or the apostles who walked with Christ, even though they make their appear-ance in a different chapter of the story. They must be filled with astonishment and gratitude and triumphant joy at the marvelous way in which God has dealt, is now dealing, and in future will deal with His people saved through the death, resurrection and ascension of Christ His Son.

How can such instruction be brought within the reach of our people? One way is to write a book dealing with these things and hope that they will read it. This book is offered to the Catholic reading public with that end in view.

But far greater numbers will be reached if priests will preach about these matters to their congregations, as the Direction of the Sacred Congregation of Rites says that they should. A second purpose of this book is, then, to help priests to fulfil this duty laid upon them by providing them with material. And as many will not have time to work up amorphous material into sermon form, I have felt it best to present what I have to offer in the shape of ready-made sermons. For this form, while being helpful to priests, is no obstacle to others who merely want to read and do not have to preach. The book can still be used as "spiritual reading" by individuals; perhaps even as table-reading in religious communities who look forward to celebrating the liturgy of Holy Week.

Some further explanation is needed, however, to account for the number and disposition of these sermons, and for the Appendices. These last, though they may perhaps interest some of the laity, are addressed explicitly to priests who are faced with sundry practical problems in carrying out the restored rites. The sermons fall into two groups of eight each for the reasons which follow.

When should priests give to their people instructions to prepare them for Holy Week? The Directive says "during the lenten season." Which means at Sunday Masses, at evening services, at daily Mass—whenever and wherever it may be possible to persuade the people to come and listen. It would surely not be too early to start even at Septuagesima, when the Church herself begins preparations for Easter.

It seems to me that our people, as regards the opportunities they will give us for imparting instruction, will fall into three classes:

(a) Those whom we shall be able to address at Sunday morning Masses only.

(b) Those who, in addition, would come to an evening service, whether on Sunday or on a week-night.

(c) Those who would come to Mass every day during Lent.

Each class will, of course, be smaller than the one before it, but, for the most part, would be contained in that class.

Those who receive the minimum instruction will be class (a). To them we can give but a sketchy outline; but I plead that it should be, as far as possible, complete. That is, it must cover the whole ground, even though details will have to be left out. The bold and clear outlines which constitute the minimum in terms of which a complete picture can be presented would comprise, it seems to me, two main themes:

(i) What God did in the past, and how this all led up to the First Coming of Christ.

(ii) What God is doing in the present, and how this will all lead up to the Second Coming of Christ.

In other words, a historical part and an eschatological part. So I have attempted to expound the former in four sermons, and the latter in four more sermons, making a basic series of eight. These are meant for use from Septuagesima Sunday to Passion Sunday inclusive. (No instruction can be given from Palm Sunday onwards because of the Holy Week services themselves.) As written they take between ten and fifteen minutes to deliver; but naturally any priest can condense or expand just as he pleases.

Some priests may think there are too many "Bible stories," especially in the first three sermons. Those who hold that view can simply leave some out. But personally I feel they are necessary.

During the period when I knew I had got to write this book but had not yet started it, I found opportunity of putting questions to various Catholic men and women of several different parishes when I was away from home preaching. The majority were people who had not had any secondary education; and I chose them deliberately as "test cases" because our congregations (at least in England) consist very largely of such people. They can more safely be taken as "average Catholics" than cultured people with secondary or university education.

In casual conversations with these people whom I had never met before, I brought the subject round to "Bible history" in order to find out what, if anything, they knew about it. Apart from one convert (ex-Methodist) they were dismally ignorant. They knew a minimum of facts (for example, that Noe went into the ark and took a lot of animals with him) but showed no vestige of any indication that there lurked, even in the innermost recesses of their minds, the slightest suspicion that these facts had any meaning. Several knew nothing at all about Abraham; others "knew not Joseph"—had never even heard of any Joseph except the Spouse of our Lady. To others Moses was only a name; "the Passover" was a word they had heard mentioned, but it meant nothing at all. "Mount Sinai" was, indeed, "a mountain in Arabia" to most of them, but about half had no idea that it had anything to do with the Ten Commandments. And so on.

I fear that we cannot take any particular person or event from the Old Testament as being generally known; some will know this, and some that—but most will be ignorant of the meaning even of what they know. That is why there is rather a lot of Bible history in the first three sermons; not for the sake of facts, but because of the meaning behind them.

It may seem also that the sermons are tiresomely repetitious. If they are read one after another, this is most certainly true, but I am inclined to think that people who hear them separated from each other by an interval of a week will not find the repetitions irksome. Where points are repeated, this is done deliberately, for the purpose of driving them home.

A certain amount of repetition is an essential ingredient of any sound teaching. If any priest thinks that his people have grasped something when he has explained it to them once, I would regard him as an optimist! Here we are concerned not with the mere presentation of facts, but with the exposition of a whole view-point; one, moreover, which is likely to be new to most of our people. Ideas do not penetrate when they are heard but once; they have to be absorbed, to grow, to take shape, to become a part of the mind. And this cannot happen unless they are presented again and again—used sometimes in combination with other ideas, sometimes in contrast—but, in any case, *used*.

The eight Sunday morning sermons will give, I hope, an understanding of the Easter Mysteries which is correct, as far as it goes, to those who receive no other instruction.

But among our Sunday morning audiences will be some who would also attend an evening instruction—either on Sunday night or on a week night. For these I have provided a second series of instructions concerned directly with the Holy Week ceremonies as such. As they consist partly of commentary on the texts of the ceremonies they are inevitably somewhat scrappy here and there, and are less suitable than the main sermons for private reading. Nevertheless I hope that ordinary readers will find in them a fair amount of interest and information. For public use, it would be well to arrange that the people should have in their hands copies of THE MASSES OF HOLY WEEK AND THE EASTER VIGIL so that they may follow the preacher's references, and have the music needed for the singing practices.

What about class (c)—those of our people who would come to daily Mass during Lent? They are likely to have attended all the other instructions because they will be the very cream of the parish—the best and most devout of our people. Though comparatively few, their quality is high; and they deserve that we should go to a good deal of trouble for their spiritual enrichment.

A very rewarding plan, which is actually carried out by a number of priests, is to make the best-attended morning Mass something very special throughout Lent. Start it five minutes earlier than usual, announcing this changed week-day time in the Sunday notices from Septuagesima onwards. Where the bishop allows it, make it a dialogue Mass; when there is a choice, always take the ferial Mass; arrange for a Lector to read out the Epistle and Gospel; and help the people to follow the entire lenten liturgy by giving them a five-minute homily every morning. Ample material can be found for this in Volume II of *The Church's Year of Grace* by Fr Pius Parsch, published by the Liturgical Press, Collegeville, Minn. For every single day the author provides abundantly. If a priest reads his Parsch each evening in preparation for next morning's Mass, he will find no difficulty whatever in talking to his people for five minutes. Such close attention to the lenten liturgy is a superb preparation for Holy Week which is itself the culmination of the whole of Lent.

To preach a short homily every morning may seem, to those who have never tried it, a formidable undertaking. But those who have done it know that it is not so difficult, and is tremendously appreciated by good people; they have found also that it is of immense benefit to themselves.

Finally it may be helpful to mention a few other books which those who can find the time would do well to read during Lent or before it. I would strongly recommend Gaillard's *Holy Week and Easter* (Liturgical Press, Collegeville, Minn.) A classic of great beauty and spiritual depth is Bouyer's *The Paschal Mystery* (Henry Regnery, Chicago). Any one who can read German should not miss Karl Becker's *Wahrhaft selige Nacht* (Herder, Freiburg). For those who read French, *La Nuit Paschale, Le Carême* and *La Baptême* (Nos. 26, 31 and 32 of *Maison Dieu*) are rich in material. The American Liturgical Conference (Elsberry, Mo.) publishes *The Easter Vigil,* the Proceedings of the 1952 Liturgical Week which was devoted wholly to a study of the Vigil. It is a truly valuable compilation.

PART ONE

Septuagesima

LET US PREPARE

You will have noticed that on this Sunday the whole mood of the Church seems suddenly to have changed; from the green vestments used for Sunday Masses since the Christmas season ended, we have now gone over to violet. And those of you who follow the text of the Mass with close attention will have observed, further, that there is no *Gloria* and that the joyous word *Alleluia* is suppressed.

All these changes are signs that we have entered upon a new phase in the Church's year; we have reached Septuagesima Sunday, which should turn our thoughts to Easter. It is, in fact, the beginning of the season of preparation for Easter.

Now Easter is not merely a date or a time; it is an *event* in the Church's year. At Easter something *happens*. That which happens—that which is the very heart of Easter—is the celebration of the *paschal Mysteries*.

As you know, the word *"paschal"* means "concerning the Pasch"; and "Pasch" is a Hebrew word which means "a passing over from slavery to freedom." The English form of it is "Passover."

And, *"Mysteries";* what are they? We usually think of a "mystery" as some truth which is beyond our understanding, but which we believe because God has told us about it. We use the word in that sense when we talk about "the mystery of the Blessed Trinity" or "the mystery of the Incarnation."

But the word has another meaning also; it means an action done by God in carrying out some plan. Thus we speak of "the mysteries of the Rosary," referring to some actions of the God-man, Christ, which we contemplate successively for the space of ten Hail Mary's. In the "Joyful Mysteries" we think over the facts that He was conceived, born, presented in the Temple, and so on. All these things He did in pursuance of a plan. So we call them "mysteries."

But Christ is still doing actions to carry out a plan, and these are also called "mysteries." He acts now in and through His Church which is His Mystical Body. The things which the Church—that is, Christ— does now are the Mass, the sacraments and the celebration of the Church's year in various ceremonies. All these are done to carry out the plan which God has devised for the purpose of getting us to heaven. Hence the Mass, the sacraments, and the celebration of the Church's year go by the name of "the Christian Mysteries." The paschal Mysteries, then, are those sacraments and celebrations which the Church does at Eastertide; they are the Mysteries concerned with the Pasch, that is, our passing from slavery to freedom, through Christ, according to the marvelous plan which the wisdom and mercy of God have brought into action.

The paschal Mysteries are the event which takes place in the Church at Eastertide. They are spread out over the whole week, beginning with the ceremony on Palm Sunday. They continue through Maundy Thursday and Good Friday, and reach their climax in the great paschal Vigil on Holy Saturday night. Especially the paschal Vigil; that is the most important of all these Mysteries. Everything else leads up to the Vigil; everything else finds its fulfilment on that "most holy night."

All these things are to be carried out by the Church this coming Easter, in pursuance of God's plan.

But you must remember that the Church does not consist merely of us clergy. The Church means *you;* you and we together form the Church of this city, this town, this neighborhood. So you and we together are to carry out the paschal Mysteries; you and we together are to work out God's plan. The paschal Mysteries must be an event, not in any vague way, but specifically for us—for our souls and minds and hearts. In us and through us and by us are these things to be done, in Christ; so that Christ, working through and in us, may bring about in our souls a further stage of His plan for our salvation.

For that is the point I would have you note carefully: your own personal participation in these holy Mysteries is a part of God's plan for you. It is not sufficient that the paschal Mysteries be celebrated; they have to be celebrated *by you* if you are to obtain their full effects. They are the means which Christ employs to pour into your souls the spiritual riches which He won for you by His passion, death and resurrection.

If you do not collaborate, then you cannot profit to the full. If you do not come to the Holy Week services, especially to the paschal Vigil, then you will miss immense opportunities of grace; your souls will be immeasurably poorer than they might have been. These services should be to you a great spiritual experience, which will instruct your minds, warm your hearts and inspire your wills. And they can be all that, provided you come to them and take part in them intelligently and with right dispositions.

In order to help you to do this, I shall devote the sermon time at Mass, for the next seven Sundays, to instructions about the meaning and purpose of the Holy Week services, especially the paschal Vigil; and the mere outline which, alone, it will be possible to give at these Masses will be amplified in further instructions to be given every Sunday (or week-night?) evening.

I appeal to you therefore, for the love of God, in gratitude to Christ our Lord, and for the sake of your own souls, to take this preparation seriously. Make a real effort to attend also the evening instructions; spend the weeks from now until Easter in the spirit which the Church desires—that of getting ready to celebrate the paschal Mysteries as well as possible.

The paschal Mysteries are, as I have said, the application to your own souls of what Christ did for you long ago. To understand them, therefore, you need to see them in their perspective; you must see, spread out before your mind's eye, the whole wonderful plan of salvation from its beginning to its end. This plan of God was in action from the earliest days of human history; it will not be completed till the end of time.

It is all centered on Christ our Lord. His passion, death, resurrection and ascension are the key to everything; but they are not of themselves everything. Part of God's plan led up to them, and another part follows them; and in this second part—without which the whole plan is not fulfilled—your annual celebration of the paschal Mysteries has a definite and important place.

We who live after Christ are in a privileged position. For we can now see the plan as a whole; it has, in fact, been revealed to us by Him. Before His time it was a kind of secret; God was at work, but men could not understand what He was doing for them. It was then, as St. Paul explained to the Romans (16:25), a "mystery, hidden from us through countless ages, but now made plain." To the Colossians he said (1:26) that it had been "a secret, hidden from all ages and generations of the past; but now He has revealed it to His saints, wishing to make known the manifold splendour of this secret among the Gentiles."

And he desired for them what I desire for you now, namely (Col. 2:2) that you may be "enriched in every way with fuller understanding, so as to penetrate the secret revealed to us by God the Father, and by Jesus Christ in whom the whole treasury of wisdom and knowledge is stored up."

Let us then try to penetrate this secret, to understand God's wonderful plan now revealed to us.

It all began with that which we priests read in our breviary prayer today—the history of creation as recounted in the Book of Genesis. God created the world and put man into it. He created Adam and Eve, and meant them to lead happy lives here, and to beget the rest of the human race who should also be happy here.

But he had something far greater in store for them. They were to remain in this world only for a while, and after that would go to be happy with God for ever in heaven. This would be perfect happiness—the same kind of happiness that God Himself has. It would far surpass anything that was possible to mere human nature. Therefore God had given to man a share in His own divine nature—that which we call "grace." Having now a share in the divine life, men would be able to share the divine happiness. That was what God intended.

But man spoiled it all. Adam, tempted by Eve, committed a sin of disobedience—the first, or "original" sin. For this, as was only just, he lost all his privileges, the chief of which was sanctifying grace. He had no longer the equipment for enjoying God's kind of happiness in heaven. He had now nothing but human life, with no share in the divine life. Moreover, he could not pass on to his children as an inheritance that which might have been theirs. He and all his race, being unequipped for heaven, could never go there.

All men were involved in his fall. "It was through one man

that guilt came into the world; and, since death came owing to guilt, death was handed on to all mankind by one man" (Rom. 6:12).

That was the ruin brought upon us by the first Adam. But at once God was ready with a plan to undo this ruin. There was to be a second Adam—another Man who would set right this wrong, who would bring to mankind not death, but life. That such a One would come was promised immediately to Adam and Eve. But He did not come immediately. Mankind was to have first of all a long preparation.

This preparation was the work of God Himself. He did it by intervening in human affairs in all sorts of ways. There came the Flood, the tower of Babel, the call of Abram, the birth of Isaac, the sale of Joseph into captivity, the appointment of Moses, the plagues of Egypt, the liberation of the Jews, the wandering in the desert, the entry into the promised land; it is an amazing and fascinating story which those who took part in it did not understand. For, although it was part of God's plan, this was still a "mystery hidden from all ages and generations of the past."

But now it is revealed for us to understand it. As St. Paul says in this morning's epistle: "Let me remind you, brethren, of this. Our fathers were hidden, all of them, under the cloud and found a path, all of them, through the sea; all alike, in the cloud and in the sea, were baptized into Moses's fellowship. They all ate the same prophetic food, and all drank the same prophetic drink, watered by the same prophetic rock which bore them company, the rock that was Christ."

There we have the point: the manna from heaven, the water from the rock, the cloud, the sea, Moses and many other persons and things in this story were all "prophetic." They were signs of persons and things to come. All of them had a meaning—hidden then, but known now. All of them led up to the coming of Christ; all were, in fact, preparations for that coming.

And if we are to understand fully all that Christ did for us and all that He is doing for us now, then we must learn the lesson of these signs and wonders of the past. For they were explanations given in advance, even though they were far from clear until Christ came.

So, just as these things prepared the Jews for the work which Christ was to do amongst them when He came in the course of history, so now the explanation of these things will prepare us for the work which Christ does amongst us when He comes in the course of Mystery—in the paschal Mysteries which we hope to celebrate together a few weeks hence. Let us, then, learn from the past, that we may profit from the future. Let us, on the next few Sundays, study these wonderful and prophetic events of the past.

Sexagesima

OF TYPES AND SYMBOLS

"Bestir Thyself, Lord . . . and awake; do not banish us from Thy presence for ever . . . prostrate, we cannot lift ourselves from the ground. Arise, Lord, help and deliver us." With those words from the Introit of today's Mass we can begin our study of what God has done to help and deliver us.

For we were, indeed, prostrate and unable to lift ourselves from the ground. Through the original sin of our first parents it seemed that we were to be banished for ever from God's presence. But no! A second Adam had been promised, and God began to prepare mankind for His coming.

In our breviary prayer today we priests read about the *story of the Flood*. A number of generations after Adam's time mankind as a whole had become very wicked. "All flesh had corrupted its way on the earth," we are told. The world needed to be cleansed from sin, so God decided to give it a good wash. He sent the great Flood.

But before doing so, He spoke to the one man who, amongst all these sinners, was still a just man. His name was Noe; God told him to build an ark, and to go into it with his family and a lot of animals. Then torrents of rain descended on the earth; the whole countryside was flooded. And, as we read in the

Bible, "the flood lifted up the ark on high from the earth, and all flesh was destroyed that moved upon the earth. And the waters prevailed upon the earth for a hundred and fifty days."

In due course the waters subsided, the ark ran aground, and God told Noe to come out of it, together with his family and the animals which had been saved. All were to be given a new chance of life. And the first thing that Noe did when he came out was to build an altar and offer a sacrifice to thank God for his safety.

And God made a promise—what the Bible calls a "covenant" —with Noe. He promised that He would never again destroy the whole of mankind with a flood, but would let nature take its course.

Now all these things "happened," as St. Paul says, "in prophecy." They were acts of God which had a meaning— which pointed to the future—even though Noe did not realize that fact. But, living in the time after Christ as we do, after the "secret has been revealed," we can see the meaning and learn the lesson if we look carefully.

For instance, this *water* of the flood was used by God to wash away sin. Can we not think of any other water, to come in the future, which is also to wash away sin? Yes, of course; the water of Baptism. The flood-water is what we call a "type," a prophetic symbol, of Baptism. Then again this flood water gave a new chance of life to men; before that men had lived a life of sin, but now Noe and his family could start a new life, a life of virtue. But that is exactly what Baptism enables us to do. We die to the old life of sin and begin a new life of grace.

Further we see that Noe and his family were saved only because they were in the *ark*. And we remember that we are saved through being in God's Church. So the ark is a "type" or prophetic symbol of the Church. The ark contained those who had been given the opportunity of a new life by the floodwaters; the Church contains those who have been given the opportunity of another life (eternal life) by the baptismal waters.

Can we see any more similarities? Surely there is another in the *covenant* which God made with Noe. That was an assurance of God's friendship, given in answer to Noe's sacrifice of thanksgiving. But we also have a sacrifice, the very name of which means "thanksgiving"; we have the sacrifice of the Eucharist. And, as we learn from the very words of consecration, it is a covenant—a "new and eternal covenant" —our perpetual assurance of God's friendship.

Let us remember these things about water and about sacrifice on Holy Saturday night; for on that night we shall be concerned with both water and sacrifice.

After a number of generations had lived and died, God went on to the next stage in the preparations for the coming of Christ, the Messiah. *God chose His ancestor in the person of Abram.* "The Lord said to Abram: go forth out of thy country and from thy kindred and come into the land which I shall show thee." So Abram (as he was called at that time) was separated off from the rest of men; he became a chosen *person*. And God promised that his descendants would be chosen *people*. "I will make of thee a great nation," said God, "and I will bless thee and magnify thy name."

Abram had a wife indeed—a very beautiful woman called Sarah; but he had no children by her as yet. However, he felt quite sure that God would fulfil his promise, and that children would be born to him in due course.

Now for many years Abram had all sorts of travels and adventures and not a few battles. One of the most important was when some neighboring tribes had carried off his nephew Lot as a prisoner. Abram, with all his followers, gave chase and rescued Lot in a fierce battle near Damascus in Syria.

When he was returning, the King of Jerusalem came to meet him. This king was called *Melchisedech,* and the remarkable thing about him is that he was also a priest. And he offered a thanksgiving sacrifice to God for Abram's victory. What do you think that he offered in sacrifice? It was bread and wine! This is the only occasion in Old Testament history when we hear of anyone offering a sacrifice with bread and wine. This was offered by one who was both king and priest. Clearly Melchisedech was a type of our Lord, the true King and true Priest, who offered the true Sacrifice of Bread and Wine which we still have with us as the Mass.

When Abram was nearly ninety years old God again promised that he would have a son. This must have seemed impossible because Sarah was now so old; yet Abram believed still that God would keep His word. What an *example of faith!*

Still nothing happened until Abram was ninety-nine years old; even then he did not get a son, but another promise. "I will make a covenant with thee," God told him, "to give thy posterity increase beyond measure." And He instituted a sign of this covenant—it was circumcision. The *covenant* was *sealed in blood!* Abram and all his people were circumcised, and by this covenant in blood they were brought into a special relationship with God, marked off as His people.

That should make us remember that we also have been brought into a special relationship with God; and this has happened because of a new covenant sealed in blood—the Blood of Christ shed upon the Cross. "This is My Blood of the new Covenant," said our Lord at the Last Supper, referring to the Blood He would shed next day.

A year after the making and sealing in blood of this covenant, God gave Abram a son, Isaac, and told the patriarch to change his own name to Abraham. This he did; and he circumcised Isaac on the eighth day.

All hopes were now centered on Isaac; from this boy would descend the great nation, the chosen people, according to God's promise. Just think how much Abraham must have loved this son of his. And yet, while Isaac was still a boy, Abraham received a most extraordinary command from God, a supreme test of his faith and obedience. God ordered him to take Isaac up onto a mountain, to build an altar there, and then to offer a *sacrifice* of his *only-begotten son!*

So strong was Abraham's faith that he would not rebel even against this hard order. He obeyed God's will though he could not understand it at all. He cut some wood and took Isaac with him; when they were going up the mountain it was Isaac who carried the wood on which he was to be sacrificed. At the top of the hill Isaac was laid upon the wood. He was the only-begotten son of his father who loved him dearly, and yet, at the bidding of that same father, he was about to die!

Is not Isaac a perfect type of our Lord who also carried up a hill the wood on which He was to be sacrificed, who also was the only-begotten Son of His Father, and who also, in accordance with the will of that same Father, was laid upon the wood to die?

In point of fact Isaac was not sacrificed after all. God intervened at the last moment, showing that what He wanted was not the life of Isaac but the generosity and *faith of Abraham*. How pleasing to God was his faith! Abraham's faith was the foundation of everything that God did for him and for his people.

That is another thing for us to remember when we celebrate the paschal Vigil; for our own faith is the foundation of everything that God has done for us; it is the first thing needed for Baptism, a sacrament which will concern us that night.

Abraham at last died; Isaac married and had two sons, Esau and Jacob; there are some very interesting stories about both of them, but we have no time to consider these now. The son who is important for our purpose is *Jacob*. To him God renewed the promise that his descendants would be the "chosen people;" and God changed his name to Israel. That is why the Jews of later days were called "the children of Israel."

Jacob had twelve sons; and the story of one of them, *Joseph,* is so interesting that I urge you very strongly to read it for yourselves out of the Book of Genesis. But now I can give the story only in outline.

Joseph was dearly loved by his father, but incurred the jealousy of his brethren. They resolved to do away with him; they stained his garments with blood, and sold him as a slave for twenty pieces of silver. Later on he was falsely accused of a crime he had not committed and was cast into prison. Then, through the providence of God, he attained to great power in the kingdom of Egypt. He did so much, not only for the Egyptians but also for other nations, that, as the Scripture says, "his name was called in the Egyptian tongue: The Savior of the World."

Now here we see a remarkable likeness to Christ our Lord. Joseph is, in fact, one of the clearest types of Christ to be found in the whole Bible. Christ also was dearly beloved of His Father; Christ's garments were stained with blood! He also was sold for pieces of silver—and by Judas, "one of the brethren." Christ also was accused of a crime He had never committed; but He ended by being the true Savior of the World.

And there is another likeness so striking that it deserves our closest attention. Joseph used his power in the land to provide bread for thousands of starving people. His servants distributed it, at his bidding, to all who came. And Christ our Lord used His power to provide bread for starving people. Think of the miracle of the feeding of the five thousand when the apostles, at His bidding, distributed the bread which sufficed for all.

And now, even in our own day, Christ is providing bread; but it is not ordinary bread for the nourishment of the body, like Joseph's bread. It is heavenly bread, the "Bread of Life," for the nourishment of the soul. The servants of Christ, who are the priests, distribute this "true bread which came down from heaven" to all who come to the altar rails for it.

Again we find something worth remembering for Holy Saturday; for the Vigil of that night will culminate in the Mass of the Resurrection—that Mass in which all should share by receiving of the Bread of Life.

With Noe, Abraham, Isaac, Jacob and Joseph we surely have enough to think about this week. We can see the beginning of God's plan for the redemption of the human race. He promised to send a Redeemer, the Messiah, and set about preparing mankind for his coming. He purged the earth by the cleansing waters and gave the human race a new life. Then he selected a man who was great in faith, and promised to make from him a chosen people to whom the Messiah should come.

Through the history of these persons God taught men about the coming Redeemer, rehearsing, as it were, the things the Redeemer would do by causing these men to do things similar in their nature or in their circumstances. These persons and their deeds were foreshadowings of the Redeemer; they were types and symbols all leading up to "Him who was to come."

By studying these men of old and their actions we are in a better position to understand God's plan, to appreciate what Christ did when He finally came, and to celebrate more fruitfully the mysteries of our redemption which we shall enact together at Eastertide.

Quinquagesima

THE PASSOVER OF THE JEWS

During the period of human history between the Fall and the Redemption God was preparing mankind for the day when He would send to them their Redeemer. Coming events were casting their shadows before them; under the providence of God various persons and happenings were pointing to the future work of Christ. For the last two Sundays we have been reviewing some of these and trying to see their meaning.

And today we shall consider the most important and instructive of all these prophecies in action; the one which will cast a flood of light not only on the Redemption as worked by Christ, but also on that celebration of it at Easter for which we are now making ready.

It is the event referred to in the Gradual of today's Mass, in which we read: "Thou art the God that alone doth work wonders; even to the Gentiles hast Thou made Thy power known. Thou hast forced them to set free Thy people, the sons of Israel and of Joseph."

When Joseph was at the height of his power, his family and relations all settled in Egypt and became prosperous there. But when Joseph had died and several generations had passed, the children of Israel had become enslaved by the Egyptians.

These Gentile masters oppressed them and reduced them to the utmost misery; they were overworked and underfed and ill treated in every possible manner. Moreover the Egyptians even decided to exterminate the Jews altogether by ordering that every male child born to them was to be cast into the River Nile.

But one of these children was saved; his name was *Moses*. He was indeed cast into the Nile, but in a floating cradle or basket, where the daughter of Pharaoh, the king, discovered him. She took pity on the baby Moses and had him brought up at court where, in the course of time, he became a great man.

But he was angered at the ill treatment of his own people, got into trouble on this account, and had to take refuge in the desert. There God appeared to him in the midst of a burning bush, and gave him orders to lead the children of Israel out of slavery into the freedom and happiness of a fertile land which God promised would some day be their home.

Again and again Moses went to Pharaoh the king of Egypt to say that God commanded the Israelites to go forth into the desert to offer sacrifice; each time Pharaoh refused, and so a terrible plague of some kind was sent upon the land. That made Pharaoh give permission; but each time he withdrew the permission as soon as the plague ceased.

Finally God decided to deliver the Israelites by a series of remarkable events which have much to teach us.

God gave orders, through Moses, that every family was to take a lamb without spot or blemish, kill it in sacrifice, and sprinkle its blood upon the door of their house. They themselves were to eat the lamb which had been sacrificed, with unleavened bread, at a ceremonial meal. That same night God would pass through the land of Egypt, and with his destroying angels would smite the Egyptians, killing the first-born of every household; but He would *pass over* the houses which had been signed with the blood of the lamb.

This night, therefore, was to be called the Passover, or Pasch; and the same name was given to the meal eaten on that occasion. This ceremonial meal was to be repeated in all its details every year in future, to commemorate the "passing over" of the Lord which enabled the Israelites to "pass over" from slavery into freedom.

For that was the result of the "passing of the Lord." "At midnight," we read in the Bible, "the Lord's stroke fell; every first-born of the land of Egypt was killed. And Pharaoh and all the Egyptians rose up, and all over Egypt there was loud lament; for in every house a man lay dead. And Pharaoh sent for Moses and his brother Aaron and said: Up,—out of my kingdom, you and all the people of Israel with you." So the people of Israel set forth.

And the Lord Himself was their guide; He went before them by day in the form of a pillar of cloud; at night it was a pillar of fire. They had but to follow the pillar and they would be on the right road to the promised land.

That is not the end of the story, but it is a convenient point at which to reflect on its meaning. Here we have again prophecy in action; these things were done to foretell the future.

The children of Israel were in slavery, but were freed through the *blood of a lamb* which was slain. Mankind was in slavery to sin, and later was to be freed through the Blood of Him whom we call "The Lamb of God"—the Messiah who was slain.

The killing of that lamb and the liberation of the people were ever afterwards to be commemorated in the *paschal meal*. And the killing of this Lamb, the Lamb of God, who liberated mankind from sin, is now for ever commemorated in a new form of the paschal meal—that which our Lord instituted at the Last Supper, itself a Pasch. The new paschal meal is, of course, the Mass, which is the Pasch of the New Testament.

Again, we see that the Israelites were being led towards their promised land by a *light* which went before them. But we, who have been freed in like manner, are also being led towards our promised land, which is heaven. And we too have a Light to guide us—Christ, the Light of the World.

When we come to celebrate the Vigil on Holy Saturday we should remember that it is a *paschal* Vigil, that is, a vigil concerned with our being set free to journey to our promised land. We shall enter into the Vigil led by a *pillar of light*—the great paschal Candle which represents Christ, the Light of the World. At the paschal Vigil we too are to have our *paschal meal;* we shall eat of unleavened bread consecrated into the very substance of the true paschal *Lamb who was slain.* We recall what St. Paul wrote: "As often as you eat this bread and drink this cup, you show forth the death of the Lord until He comes."

Now let us resume the story. Led by the pillar of cloud or of fire the Israelites came to the shores of the Red Sea. Pharaoh, discovering that they had escaped during the night, pursued them with all his chariots and his entire army. But God caused the waters to part, standing up like a wall on either side of a path over which the Israelites *passed over* to the other shore. Then, when the Egyptians were half way over, the waters returned to their place and drowned them all.

Like the waters of the Flood which we thought about last Sunday, these waters were the means of life to some, and of death to others. It was by *passing through the waters* that the Israelites were enabled to begin a new life. Consequently these waters, like those of the Flood, are a type of the sacrament of Baptism. In fact they are a more perfect type because they led up directly to more divine actions which, in their turn, are themselves types of those mysteries of Christ which follow Baptism. Let us see what these are.

Up till this time the Israelites, as slaves of the Egyptians, had been a disordered mob with no constitution of their own, being subject to the laws of their oppressors. But now that they had passed through the waters, God fulfilled the promise, made so long ago to Abraham and renewed to Isaac and Jacob, that their progeny should be a nation or a *people*.

God called them to Mount Sinai that they might hear His word; He called Moses to Him and said: "Tell them: You are to keep a covenant with Me; and I, to whom all the earth belongs, will single you out among its peoples to be my own people. You shall serve Me as a *royal priesthood,* as a *consecrated people*. Tell the Israelites this" (Ex. 19:5).

Those who had passed through the waters were thus aggregated into a chosen people, subject to God's laws.

But that is precisely what happens in Baptism. It makes us members of God's chosen people of the New Testament—those to whom St. Peter referred when he said: "You are a chosen race, a royal priesthood, a consecrated nation . . . Time was when you were not a people at all, but now you are God's people" (1 Pet. 2:9, 10).

And those newly constituted people of the Old Testament made answer to God's word; the Bible says "they answered with one voice: We will do all that the Lord has said." This was the covenant with God; they would observe His laws, and God would cherish them as His own chosen people.

And the covenant was confirmed in *sacrifice*. For Moses at once built an altar and sacrifice was offered: "Moses poured blood over the altar, and sprinkled the people with the blood, crying out: Here is the blood of the covenant which the Lord makes with you" (Ex. 24:6, 8).

But so it is with the new chosen people of God, the baptized. They too accept God's laws; they too are cherished by God as His own people; they too come to an altar to offer sacrifice; and this also is a sacrifice in blood. "This is My Blood," said Christ when He instituted it; "My Blood of the new and everlasting covenant."

All this will happen over again *to us* at the paschal Vigil. We shall listen to God's word; we shall answer with one voice: "We will do all that the Lord has said." For that is what we mean at the renewal of our baptismal vows. We shall renew also our covenant with God to be His chosen people, and this will be confirmed in the Sacrifice of the New Covenant which concludes the Vigil.

Thinking again of the old chosen people, we remember another type, fulfilled now in us. God fed his people as they journeyed towards their promised land. He rained down *bread from heaven* having in it all manner of sweetness. This bread, which they called Manna, is a type of the Blessed Sacrament, the true Bread from heaven. God gives it to us to be the food of our souls as we journey towards our promised land. The Manna was only for the old chosen people who had passed through the waters—no one else might have it. The Eucharist is only for the new chosen people who have passed through the waters of Baptism—no one else may have it.

Further, God willed that the old chosen people should build Him a house for worship; there was to be an altar in it; certain men were to be consecrated as priests, and should wear special garments when officiating at the altar. Incense was to be burned, holy oils were to be used, precious vessels of gold and silver should be set aside for the worship of God. "And the Lord said to Moses: Give the sons of Israel a warning from Me. Be sure that you observe the Sabbath Day. It is a token between us, reminding you that I am the Lord, and you are set apart for me" (Ex. 31:12).

It is quite plain how all these things apply, but in a new way, to us who are God's chosen people of the New Testament. They are, in fact, types of what we have in the Church now.

By now you can surely grasp, at least in broad outline, the plan which God was carrying out in the course of all this history. He kept shaping human affairs with the definite purpose of preparing for the coming of the Redeemer. The preparations had a definite form, namely, the constitution of a chosen people, linked with God by a covenant, worshiping Him in sacrifice, celebrating their freedom by a prescribed ritual, destined for a promised land, and ever looking forward to the coming of their Messiah. Moreover all these things were done in a definite manner—namely, by way of signs and wonders and persons and events which had a meaning. This meaning was hidden at the time, but was revealed by Christ for whom all this had been a preparation.

The more clearly you grasp this, the more fully you will realize the import of all that Christ our Lord actually did when this preparatory period in the history of our salvation was terminated by His coming.

First Sunday of Lent

THE PASSOVER OF CHRIST

So far we have been thinking over God's dealings with mankind in Old Testament days; and we have seen that all this history was a preparation for the coming of Christ. What Christ would do was, so to speak, rehearsed in a prophetic and symbolic way. The children of Israel were freed from slavery by the blood of the paschal lamb; they passed over through the waters; they were made into a chosen people and set on their way to a promised land.

Now this Sunday we come to the *fulfilment* of all these types and figures in the redemption worked for us by Christ. He is the true Paschal Lamb by whose Blood we have been freed; we have passed through the waters of Baptism and have become a new chosen people on the way to a new promised land, which is heaven.

Our liberation from sin and death—that is, our salvation—has moreover the same form as the historic liberation of the Jews. It is, in fact, a passover. And we are enabled thus to pass over from a state of bondage to freedom, from death to life, only because Christ came, and Himself passed over this very way before us. What He did for us during His mortal life is, in its essence, a passover.

Being human, we can only think in a human way about God's plan for saving mankind. It would seem to us that the fall of man confronted God with a problem. Here was man, down below, in a world of sin and death; there was God, up above, in everlasting life and happiness. God's problem, if we may express it so, was how to get poor man, subject to misery and death, into His own kingdom of happiness and life.

And He solved the problem by sending down the second Person of the Blessed Trinity into this world to become a man. Now there would be, even in this world of sin and death, a man who was God. All other men were quite incapable of passing over the gulf which separated earth from heaven. But this Man, being God, would have the power to do so.

He would, then, pass over the gulf, returning to His Father and resuming His former glory; but He would not return alone. Having gone down into the world He would, as it were, take hold of men and make them His very own; so that, by adhering to Him they too would be able to pass over, as He had passed over, from the world of darkness to that of light, from the kingdom of death to that of life.

If Christ had been concerned merely with His own return to the Father from out of this world, He could have done without any suffering and without death. His personal passover could have consisted only of ascension and enthronement at the Father's right hand.

But, as the Nicene Creed reminds us, it was "for us men and for our salvation" that He descended from heaven. He chose, therefore, a way of return to His Father which was in accordance with our position rather than with His.

We are sinful men, barred from eternal life by the consequences of rebellion against God. By sin we are attached to creatures; we cannot go to God unless we are torn loose from them—and that is a process involving pain. The path of sinful man towards God is not only a path which man is unable to traverse by his own powers; it is one which, even if he be dragged along it by the power of Another, necessarily involves suffering.

That is why the sinless Man Christ, who could have attained to God without any suffering, nevertheless chose the *path of suffering* because that path is the only possible way for men who are sinful. It was through His Passion and Cross that He decided to return to His Father, to pass over from this world to that. He, who was in truth God's Son, took upon Himself the form of a slave, making Himself in all things like to us, sin alone excepted. Though utterly guiltless, He chose the way of the guilty, in order that those who were guilty might themselves be drawn along that same way with Him and in Him.

Thus the passover of the sinless Christ could become the passover of His sinful brethren in the flesh; they too, through His Passion, Death, Resurrection and Ascension, would be able to make their way to God.

But all this is possible for them only on condition that they become in some way *attached to Christ* by a bond so strong that His going to heaven involves their going to heaven. Unless they be joined to Him, the mere fact that Christ returned to His glory through suffering and death would not profit them. Even though going by the path proper to sinful man, He would be going alone. He might just as well have returned to His Father by mere ascension, without any passion and death, unless men are united with Him so as to be carried along with Him.

So we see that the plan of God involved also a further task for Christ to perform while He was on earth; this was the provision of means whereby men could enter into vital relationship with Him; it was a forging of a bond between Himself and them, a bond so intimate that His actions could become their actions, His passover could become their passover, His glory could become their glory.

Having provided for men the means of union with Him, He could then pass to His glory, leaving it possible for men to make use of those means whereby, in union with Him, they too could make the journey from death to life, from earth to heaven.

What Christ did to effect this was foreshadowed by what God did to bring the Jews of old to their promised land. They were set free by the blood of a lamb that was offered in sacrifice; then they were led through the waters and formed into a chosen people on the march to their goal.

And now the same thing has happened all over again for us, not in figure but in fact. We have been set free by the Lamb of God offered in sacrifice; and we also have been led through waters (of Baptism), and formed into a new chosen people on the march to our goal.

But we are more than a chosen people on the march; we are also the Mystical Body of Christ. Our Savior has made us so one with Himself that we can travel with Him and in Him. He was not only the true Paschal Lamb whose blood set us free; He was also the Second Adam whose destiny involves our destiny, just as the destiny of the First Adam in his fall involved us too.

For Christ has a dual role. The paschal lamb typifies only part of His redemptive work. The original paschal lamb was slaughtered, but did not conquer death by rising again. Christ fulfilled the prophetic fate of the paschal lamb by His dying; but in His rising He acted as the Second Adam undoing the work of the First Adam. "A man brought us death," says St. Paul (1 Cor. 15:21), "and a man was to bring us resurrection from the dead. Just as all have died with Adam, so with Christ all will be brought to life." "Adam was the type of Him who was to come. If this one man's fault brought death on a whole multitude, all the more lavish was God's grace . . . brought by one man, Jesus Christ" (Rom. 5:15).

"You know well enough," St. Paul continues, "that we who were taken up into Christ by baptism have been taken up, all of us, into his death . . . We have to be closely fitted into the pattern of his resurrection, as we have been into the pattern of His death . . . If we have died with Christ, we have faith to believe that we shall share His life."

It is, then, by Baptism that we are "taken up" into the death and also into the resurrection of Christ. By passing through the waters of Baptism we are made members of His chosen people, of His Church. We have risen with Him and share His life, so that we belong to Him as a body belongs to its head. For "He is the head to which the whole Church is joined, so that the Church is His body" (Eph. 1:22).

Now we can see how it is that the passover of Christ from earth to heaven can become the passover of us sinful men. The destiny of the Head is the destiny of the Body. If we are of the Body, we can share the glory of the Head. The work Christ did for our redemption consists not merely in dying as the true Paschal Lamb, but in rising as the Second Adam; not merely in freeing us from Satan but in uniting us to Himself.

It is quite inadequate to see in our redemption nothing but the fact that "we were bought with a great price"—the price which is the Blood of God's Son shed upon the Cross. It is, of course, perfectly true that we were so purchased—St. Peter reminds us of the fact in so many words. But if we limit our gaze to this fact alone, we see only one aspect of our redemption. This alone leads to a distorted view—as if we had been the subject of some kind of barter between God and the Devil.

The same may be said of that view which sees in the Passion only a reparation with respect to God, accomplished by the sinless Man Christ on behalf of His sinful fellow-men. That also is true as far as it goes; but it does not go far enough. No view of the Passion and Death of Christ goes far enough except that which penetrates right past them to the Resurrection,

Ascension and Sitting at the right hand of the Father. For the whole work of Christ is a passover which is aimed at and actually terminates in His return to the Father in glory.

The mystery of Christ, then, consists in this: in His own right He was not liable to death. But He chose to return to His Father by way of death because that is the penalty to which all His brethren in the flesh were liable on account of sin. In taking this dolorous path He thereby blazed the trail; by His divine power He burst the bonds of death in which all other men were held fast. By founding His Church with her power to baptize, He rendered it possible for men to enter into vital union with Him; they could become members of His Body, they could "put on Christ," so that by His power and in His victory they could travel with Him along this same path through death and resurrection unto glory.

The harm which the First Adam had wrought under the Tree of Paradise was set right by the Second Adam on the Tree of the Cross, so that those who had to die because of the physical relationship to the First Adam would be enabled to rise because of their spiritual relationship to the Second Adam. Thus the passover of Christ from earth to heaven would be reproduced in those who had become His own.

"Before the paschal feast began," wrote St. John, "Jesus already knew that the time had come for his passage from this world to the Father" (John 13:1). By that passage of Christ, foreshadowed in the historic passover of the Jews, was rendered possible the passover of those whom He redeemed.

It is only through Him and with Him and in Him that we can pass over from the slavery of sin and death to the everlasting kingdom of grace and of life. Indeed, when we see all that this means for us, we can understand the words which our risen Lord spoke to the disciples on the way to Emmaus: "Was it not *necessary* that Christ should undergo these sufferings, and so enter into his glory?"

Second Sunday of Lent

THE PASSOVER OF CHRISTIANS

The account of our Lord's Transfiguration which we read in today's Gospel should help to bring home to us the truth of one point we considered last Sunday, namely, that the state of glory belonged to Christ by right; had He been concerned only for Himself He could have enjoyed not merely transfiguration here below whenever He wanted, but could also have returned to His Father in heavenly glory without undergoing death.

But He deliberately chose to pass over from earth to heaven by the way of suffering and death for our sakes because that was the only possible way for sinful men whom He desired to draw after Him.

And now He was revealing this intention to His apostles; for in St. Luke's account of the Transfiguration we are told that He spoke to Moses and Elias "of the death which He was to achieve in Jerusalem"; and afterwards "He warned them," as today's Gospel says, "Do not tell anybody of what you have seen until the Son of Man has risen from the dead." His death was not going to be a defeat; it would be followed by resurrection and a triumphant return—a passover—to His Father's side.

But all this would be the culmination of a long period of preparation. As we have seen in the previous weeks, there had been a continual intervention of God in human affairs.

It began with God's promise that a Savior would indeed come. But before He did come, all sorts of things happened. Remember the waters of the Flood, the covenant of circumcision, the sacrifice of Isaac, the betrayal of Joseph, the slaying of the paschal lamb, the liberation of Israel, the passage through the Red Sea, the wandering in the desert, the manna—there was type after type, wonder after wonder, sign after sign, whereby the chosen people were constituted and prepared for the coming of the Messiah.

Then at last He came. He worked our redemption. Then He went back to heaven. But this is not the end of His activity among men. For, before He ascended to heaven, He said that He would come back again. There is to be a Second Coming of Christ.

Wherefore the whole process begins as it were all over again. As there is another promise of "Him who is to come," there is likewise another preparation for His coming. There are more signs and wonders. There are more waters to wash away sin— but this time they are the waters of Baptism. There is a new chosen people of God—this time ourselves. There is a new wandering in the desert—this time it is the desert of our earthly life. There is a new covenant in Blood, and a new Bread from heaven—this time the Mass and the Eucharist.

All these signs and wonders are taking place now, in our own day; and they are preparing us, the new chosen people of God, for the second coming of Christ, just as the signs and wonders of old prepared the former chosen people for the first coming of Christ.

Only when He comes again will human history be finished; only then will God's plan for the salvation of mankind be brought to its triumphant conclusion.

Human history is, as it were, in two chapters. In the first chapter real people (such as Abraham and Melchisedech and David and Josue) did signs and wonders which led up to the first coming of Christ. And in the second chapter, which is going on now, real people (such as our Holy Father the Pope, Bishop A, Father B, Mr. C, Mrs. D, and you and I) are doing the signs and wonders which will lead up to the second coming of Christ.

Their signs were in water (as of the Red Sea) and oil (as of Aaron) and bread (as of Melchisedech) and song (as of David); but our signs also are in water (as of Baptism) and oil (as of Confirmation) and bread (as of the Eucharist) and song (as of the divine office). Our place in the history of salvation is just as real as theirs; but our signs and wonders are even more real than theirs.

For their signs did but look forward to ours; their signs were the types, ours the *realities* which they prefigured. Their signs merely signified; ours *effect* what they signify. For our signs were instituted by Christ at His first coming, for the express purpose of making us ready for His second coming. Ours are the signs and wonders of Christ—the "Mysteries of Christ" as they are called. Another name for them is the Mass and the sacraments—in fact all that is comprised in the term "liturgy."

What Christ did at His first coming was "the work of our redemption." He did all things necessary to make it possible for us to reach heaven. This is called "objective redemption." But His doing all that does not mean that we necessarily *shall* reach heaven. As the Pope says in the encyclical *Mediator Dei,* "in order that the redemption of individuals in all ages till the end of the world may become effective, it is necessary for each to get vitally in touch with the sacrifice of the Cross."

This getting in touch with the sacrifice of the Cross is called "subjective redemption"; it is the work of Christ *in you and me*. Objective redemption is what He did two thousand years ago in Palestine; subjective redemption is what He does in Chicago or in our own town today in you and me. It is still "the work of our redemption." It makes us ready for His second coming which will complete all His redemptive work.

Objective redemption was worked by Him alone; but subjective redemption needs our active collaboration—for it consists in those signs and wonders which He instituted—those "mysteries of Christ" which are the liturgy and in which we must take part. For, to quote the Pope again, "the work of our redemption is continued and its fruits are imparted to us by the celebration of the liturgy."

This is so because unless Christ had devised some way for us to attain to union in Him, His passover from earth to heaven could not profit us. He, as the Son of God, would have returned to His Father alone. But if His passover is to become our passover, if His entrance into glory is to be our entrance into glory, then there must be some way in which His actions can become our actions. Accordingly He devised a way in which that can be so.

His way was to form us into a new chosen people so intimately sharing His own divine life as to be a Body in which He continues to live and be active. That Body is His Church in which He now lives and acts, in which He now works our subjective redemption. It is called His Mystical Body to distinguish it from the physical Body in which He formerly lived and worked our objective redemption. This Mystical Body is formed of the new chosen people.

There are many similarities between the old chosen people and the new. The old chosen people were those who had passed through the waters of the Red Sea; the new chosen people are those who have passed through the waters of Baptism. The old chosen people celebrated every year the Pasch, which was a prescribed ritual looking back to the occasion when they were freed, but also looking forward to the coming of the Savior. The new chosen people is likewise to celebrate every year a Pasch; and this Pasch is also a prescribed ritual looking back to the occasion when they were freed, while at the same time looking forward to the coming of the Savior.

Those are similarities. But much more important are the differences.

They of old looked forward to the first coming of the Savior; we look forward to His second coming. They looked back to a Passover and a paschal lamb which were mere types; we look back to a Passover and to a Paschal Lamb which were fulfilments. Their ritual celebration was prescribed by Moses, a mere figure of Christ. Our ritual celebration was prescribed by Christ Himself.

Their paschal supper had no reality beyond its ritual—it was only a memory and a prefigurement. But our paschal supper has a reality underlying its ritual; like the other, it looks back and it looks forward—but in addition to that it also *makes present*. It recalls Christ's passover gone by and it prefigures our own passover to come, but also it *contains within itself* the mysterious presence and power of that passover which it symbolizes. For our paschal supper is none other than the Mass—the center and summit of the Christian mysteries.

The new chosen people of God exists, therefore, not for its own sake but for the purpose of effecting the work of subjective redemption in its members. It is the divine organism which celebrates the paschal Mysteries. The Mass is the primary paschal Mystery, of which the Church herself says "every offering of this memorial sacrifice carries on the work of our redemption" (Secret, ninth Sunday after Pentecost).

But all the rest of the liturgy is centered round or directed to this paschal Mystery; the sacraments are like planets which all revolve round that sun which is the Mass. It is through them that men are born and aggregated to the Church and equipped with the powers needed for the celebration of Mass. We may say that the other sacraments are there in order that there may be a Church capable of offering Mass; for the Mass, which is the celebration of the paschal Mysteries, is the chief way in which the objective redemption is worked out in men subjectively, so that the passover of Christ can become the passover of men.

Precisely how this is so is beyond our understanding; but there are certain aspects of it that we can grasp. The Mass is the act of Christ. It is celebrated in order that we may share in it, in order that we as His members may have a part in it and be united to Christ's redemptive work.

The work of our redemption is rendered actual, not in historic form but in sacramental form. The passover of Christ which took place in Palestine two thousand years ago becomes the passover of His members in this or that place today because they have part in its sacramental celebration.

It was then that He died and rose again and entered into glory; it is now that we die in Him, rise in Him, and derive from Him that supernatural life which is the beginning of our own glory.

The glory which will one day be ours through the celebration of these Mysteries is the same glory which is already His; it will be the eternal Pasch celebrated by the chosen people in their promised land of heaven—that which St. John described in his apocalyptic vision as the Feast of the Lamb, immolated and glorious.

That will explain why the Easter celebrations for which we are now preparing are all grouped about and centered on the Mass. The triumphal procession in honour of Christ the King which opens the whole week is followed by the Mass. On Maundy Thursday the celebration is itself a Mass with other features attached to it.

On Good Friday the whole point of the celebration is the

very fact that it is not a Mass; we devote ourselves not to the mystic renewal of our redemption but solely to the memory of its historic occurrence.

But then, on Holy Saturday Night we have the greatest celebration of all—that which is most explicitly concerned with the paschal Mysteries as such. We have a vivid recalling of the passover of the old chosen people; then we proceed to the paschal sacrament (Baptism) which constitutes the new chosen people; and we bring it to a conclusion with the Pasch of the New Covenant which is the Mass. We say with St. Paul, "Christ our Pasch is sacrificed."

And by all these celebrations, the work of our redemption is continued and applied to us subjectively. We grow in Christ and Christ grows in us, so that our vital union with Him will cause His passover to become our passover. We prepare for His second coming at which all these signs will give way to their fulfilment and we shall enjoy with Him that eternal Pasch in our promised land for which the whole work of redemption has been accomplished.

Third Sunday of Lent

THE PASCHAL VIGIL

The Christian religion is not a mere collection of doctrines, nor even of moral precepts; it is a great action, uniting men to God through Christ the One Mediator.

It is an action, of which the beginning was the first coming of Christ, and of which the end will be the second coming of Christ. And in between these two comings, the work of Christ is ever continued among men by the celebration of the Christian Mysteries in His Church which is His Mystical Body.

The whole saving action of Christ may be summed up in the word "passover"; at His first coming He passed, by way of His passion, death, resurrection and ascension to His Father. And ever since then the Church has preached and celebrated this passover of Christ, in order that it may become also the passover of men; she will continue to do this "until He comes."

When the Apostles first went forth to preach, this was the burden of their message. St. Peter, on the Day of Pentecost, proclaimed that He whom the Jews had crucified had now risen again. To the crowds that gathered about him in the Temple a few days later he asserted: "You killed the Author of life, but God has raised Him up again from the dead." When arrested and brought before the rulers of the Jews, Peter and John boldly declared the resurrection. After their escape from prison they were found again preaching in the Temple and again it was of the resurrection that they spoke.

It is the same with all the other Apostles of whose preaching we have any record—constantly they were stressing the fact that Christ had conquered death.

And there were many who believed and were baptized. Baptism, the first of the Christian Mysteries, brought a continual increase to the Church. And straightway we hear of the Church doing that for which she exists, namely, celebrating the Mass, which is the Christian pasch.

In what spirit did the early Christians do this? In a spirit of *reminiscence:* they were fulfilling the command of Christ who had said, "Do this in memory of Me." In a spirit of *union:* "they were persevering in the doctrine of the Apostles and in the communication of the breaking of bread" (Acts 2:42). In the spirit of *expectation:* they were looking and longing for the second coming of Christ. "As often as you eat this bread and drink this chalice," St. Paul told them, "you show forth the death of the Lord until He come" (1 Cor. 11:27).

The expectation that Christ would come again was very strong in the early Church. Indeed no one knew exactly when He would come, but most of them seem to have thought that He would come quite soon. They had a name for the great day of His coming—the *"Parousia."* Because of His parable of the Bridegroom who came at midnight, the prevailing opinion was that the Parousia was likely to occur at that hour, or else in the early dawn when He had risen from the dead.

It was early on Sunday that He rose; it was early on Sunday that He had visited His apostles; hence an early hour on Sunday was deemed the most fitting time for the celebration of the Christian Mysteries.

But because they desired to be ready for the Parousia, and to be found awake watching for their Master like the good servant in His parable, they used to meet on Saturday night and pass the time in prayer and reading of the holy Scriptures until they celebrated the Mass as dawn approached.

Sunday, then, was the Lord's Day for the early Church. Every Sunday, after a vigil during the previous night, they celebrated the events of Easter, the passover of their Lord. Every Sunday, in fact, was a little Easter, a passover wherein they made the passover of Christ their own, showing forth the death of the Lord until He should come. Sunday was *the* Christian feast day; in fact for several generations it was the only Christian feast day. They had no feast but a paschal feast—and that they celebrated every week.

But as time went on it was natural that they should give special prominence to one of these weekly paschal feasts—that one, in fact, which corresponded in date with the original happenings celebrated.

This tendency became apparent first of all in Jerusalem where the celebration by the Jews of the ancient pasch caused the Christians to react by laying special emphasis on that celebration of the Christian pasch which occurred at the same time. Thus there arose a definite Feast of Easter; it was considered the principal feast, of which all other Sundays were an echo.

But still this was a unitive feast, the subject of which was not just the resurrection, but the *entire* passover of Christ. His passion, death, resurrection and ascension were still considered as so many phases of one act—His passage from this sinful world to the world of glory. Thus Easter was the foundation-feast of the Church; it brought to mind the basic facts on which the very existence and life of the Church rested.

By the third century there was a further development, again starting in Jerusalem and spreading gradually throughout the Christian world.

As it was in Jerusalem that the events of the redemption

happened, the custom grew of celebrating the various episodes on the very spot where they had taken place, and on the anniversaries of their first occurrence. The feast of Easter became, as it were, enlarged and spread out. Only the resurrection was celebrated on Easter Sunday; the passion and death were recalled on the previous Friday, the Last Supper and Betrayal on Thursday, and, in course of time, even the solemn entry into Jerusalem was re-enacted on the Sunday before Easter.

Thus there came into being all of Holy Week as we know it now. But still Easter, in this expanded form, was the only feast of the Christian year; and the Saturday night vigil, culminating in the Mass of the Resurrection towards the dawn of Easter Sunday, was still the climax of the whole. All the other celebrations were but preparatory.

It was later still that the Ascension, and then Pentecost, began to have days of their own, calculated from the date of Easter.

And because none of these things could have happened unless Christ had entered this world, there was instituted—first in Asia Minor and subsequently in other places—a feast of the Incarnation. This, too, began as a unitive feast of which the content was the Manifestation of God to man in the Person of Christ. By the fourth century this general idea had become analyzed into these constituents which we now celebrate on December 25 and January 6 respectively—the two feasts of Christmas and Epiphany.

Thus we see that Christmas, regarded by many now as the greatest feast of the year, is in point of fact quite subsidiary. Christmas, Epiphany, Ascension, Pentecost and all the other feasts we now have were all evolved in dependence on Easter— either as preparations for it, or as prolongations of its content.

The fact is, then, that Easter is the greatest of all feasts, and that the paschal Vigil is the summit and center of the Easter celebrations themselves. There is no church service in the entire year, therefore, which is as important as that for which we are now preparing by this course of sermons.

That we may understand it better and come to it with more fully prepared minds, let us trace out a little further the development of this all-important function.

The resurrection of Christ took place in the early hours of the morning, towards sunrise. Hence the rising of Christ was likened to the rising of the sun which brought the long night to its end. Pagans used to worship the sun; Christians therefore regarded Christ whom they worshipped, as the True Sun.

According to the old ideas, the sun, at its setting in the west, used to go down into the earth and travel through the underworld to emerge next morning in the east. So the Christians saw the death and burial of Christ as the setting of the True Sun who descended into the underworld of Limbo. After visiting the patriarchs and holy men of old who were waiting there, the True Sun rose again in brilliance and glory on Easter morning.

But the sun is the light of this world; and they remembered that Christ had said of Himself that He was the Light of the World. Simeon had proclaimed Him as the Light to be revealed to the Gentiles, and St. John, at the beginning of his Gospel, had written of Him as "the true light which illuminates every man born into the world."

It seemed therefore both natural and fitting to celebrate the redemption by a *night watch* wherein darkness would be overcome by light, just as the long night of sin was brought to an end by the rising of the True Sun, Christ, from under the earth.

These ideas led to another. Christ was not a light who shone for Himself; He shone for others, to communicate His light to them. And the light of Christ is communicated to men through the teaching of His Church. It is only by entrance into the Church of Christ that men can be flooded by the light of Christ.

Wherefore, by the second century, there had grown the custom of admitting to the Church, during the holy paschal night, those who had been seeking admission. The sacrament of admission to the Church, which is *Baptism,* was thus the sacrament which brought illumination by the light of Christ. In fact at this period Baptism was called "the Enlightenment"; and the baptized were referred to as "those who had been enlightened." The lighted candle given to the newly baptized is a reminder to us even now of this beautiful thought.

Besides the idea of enlightening, which indicates the paschal Vigil as a pre-eminently suitable occasion for administering Baptism, there was another thought in the Christian mind. St. Paul had described Baptism as a *burial with Christ and a rising with Christ* to new life. And as the ceremony of Baptism in those days involved a descent into, and an emergence from, a bath set below ground level, the analogy with the descent of Christ into His tomb and subsequent resurrection was striking. So here was an additional reason for administering Baptism during the paschal Vigil: on no other occasion could its symbolism and full meaning stand out so clearly for all to grasp.

There is one more factor which contributed to the content of the paschal Vigil, namely, the *reading of the holy Scriptures.* Public reading was very important in those days when books—all of them hand-written—were rare and expensive, and when so many people were illiterate. There was no more fitting way of passing the time in church than to listen to the reading of Scripture passages chosen to suit the occasion. After each extract that was read there followed normally the singing of a *Psalm or Canticle,* in which the people joined by interpolating a short chorus after each verse. This, in turn, was followed by a *prayer,* sung by the celebrant, and answered by all the people in their acclamation *"Amen."*

In the course of time these readings for the paschal Vigil

became twelve in number; they were from the Old Testament and traced out broadly the history of God's preparations for the redemption now being celebrated on that night. Thus were evolved what have come to be called "the prophecies."

But one could not read the Scriptures without light. So the service began with the *lighting of a candle* for the deacon who was to read; naturally this candle was blessed; and the solemn blessing given to it and to its light developed gradually into that wonderful song which remains with us in the form of the *Exsultet*. And from this in turn grew all the other ceremonies concerned with fire and light and the spreading of light which now form the first part of the service.

To sum up, then: the great Easter festival is nowadays spread over a whole week, but its climax is the Holy Saturday Vigil. It consists of a Night Watch, held in memory of the first coming of the Lord, and in expectation of His second coming. The contents of the night watch are made up of a festival of light, followed by Scripture reading, song and prayer; then comes a baptismal celebration; and this culminates in a Mass of the Resurrection, early on the Sunday morning, in fulfillment of all the basic ideas underlying the various parts of the vigil. That is a brief account of the origin and meaning of the paschal Vigil. We shall examine it more in detail later.

Fourth Sunday of Lent

THE SPIRIT OF THE VIGIL

The great Easter Vigil, of which the origin and content was explained to you in outline last Sunday, though in reality the most important of all the ceremonies in the Church's year, came in the course of history to suffer serious neglect. There were many causes contributing to this.

One was the fact that adult Baptisms became rare, and infant Baptisms the norm. Hence the practice of baptizing at the Vigil gradually died out and there remained nothing of the baptismal celebrations except the blessing of the font.

In consequence the Vigil, begun in the evening, was shorter than it used to be and ended earlier—at midnight or even before midnight. This obscured the idea of watching during the night—of deliberately being awake while the rest of the world was asleep. The service, instead of being understood as a purposeful avoidance of sleep, began to be regarded as an interference with sleep; and so it was drawn forward into the early evening, or even the afternoon in order that it might not interfere with sleep.

Thus the Mass which concluded it began to have a position like all the other Masses of the lenten season, namely in the afternoon. These were in the afternoon because the days of Lent were all fast days; the fast might not be broken until after the official prayer of None, the proper time for which was, according to our modern reckoning, 3 p.m. The Mass was celebrated after None because of the notion—rather curious to our way of thinking—that to receive holy Communion was to break the fast. But by the fourteenth century the spirit of penance had so diminished that men would no longer fast so late. The prayer of None was therefore pushed forward into the morning and followed by Mass, so that the fast could then be broken in the morning.

Because all the other lenten Masses were now brought forward to the morning, the same thing was done to the Holy Saturday Mass. As it had long been celebrated about the same time as the other Masses it had become classified with them. Thus it, too, became a morning Mass in order that the fast might end earlier. And that meant that all the ceremonies which preceded it were done in the morning—even in the early morning.

This went on for several centuries; and the fact that the early hour was completely at variance with the spirit of these ceremonies did not much disturb people who had to a large extent lost a true appreciation of the Church's official worship.

In our own day there has been a happy awakening. During the past half century there has been a growing number of people, both clergy and laity, who have realized that we cannot afford to treat as mere ritual that which enshrines the very life of the Church herself, namely, the liturgy.

The liturgical movement of modern times is filled with a *spirit of sincerity*. It strives to make dead ritual into living and meaningful worship, to live the life of the Church according to the mind of the Church as expressed in the words of the liturgy, to pray the Church's prayers in sincerity and in truth.

Those caught in this movement found it disconcerting in

the extreme that the priest should bless on Holy Saturday *morning* a fire which he was bidden to call a *"nocturnal flame"*; that the deacon should call on God to "dissipate the darkness of this night" at a time when the sunlight of a spring morning was streaming through the church windows; or that he should express the hope that "this temple may echo with the multitude's full-throated song" when, by reason of the early hour, the only "multitude" which could be there would amount to a handful of women and children and perhaps a couple of old men.

There arose a widespread dissatisfaction with this state of affairs, and an earnest desire that this lovely and meaningful service might be restored to its proper time during the night, when its words could be spoken and sung with realism, and when the people, unimpeded by their daytime work, would be free to take part in it.

Pope Pius XII has graciously listened to the plea of his earnest children; and in 1951 he not only permitted the Vigil to be restored to its rightful hour, but even caused it to be revised and reformed in accordance with the needs of our own day.

A similar process of displacement overtook the other Holy Week ceremonies; the Mass of Holy Thursday, as a commemoration of the Last Supper, used to be in the evening, and the Good Friday ceremony, commemorating our Lord's death on the Cross used to be in the afternoon. But in the course of time both of these were drawn forward into the morning and thereby lost much of their significance. In 1955 the Holy Father restored them both to their proper times, and confirmed the restored Vigil by promulgating the Reformed Order of Holy Week.

It is a wonderful gift that he has given to us, and we have a duty of gratitude to profit by it to the full. But we can do that only if we take part in it with deep understanding.

There are many people, alas, even among those who make use of the Restored Vigil, who lack this understanding. They have missed the point. They imagine that the reason for putting the service into the evening is that it may end with a Midnight Mass. We have a Midnight Mass at Christmas because we believe that Christ was born about midnight. Just so, according to this view, we now have a Midnight Mass at Easter because Christ must have risen not long after midnight. But that is not the point at all.

The real point is not that we have a Mass, but that we have a *vigil*. This vigil, this night watch, is of a nature such that it demands the celebration of the Christian Mysteries, the Mass, as its climax. The authentic celebration of the paschal Mysteries does not consist, then, in having a Mass, however picturesque. Its essence is to keep a vigil—and the final element of the vigil is the Mass.

Ideally the vigil should last—and in the early Church it did last—throughout the whole night, from dusk to dawn. But the central idea remains intact so long as we do have a genuine vigil, even in shortened form, to carry us through from Holy Saturday to Easter Sunday.

The proper time for the Vigil service is, therefore, that which will bring the beginning of the Mass somewhere about midnight. But experience in the past few years has shown that in some places this late hour gives rise to very real difficulties for the people. They may have a very long way to come to church and lack transport which would be available earlier in the evening. And since the motive of the reform is, above all else, pastoral, these facts have to be taken into account. It is more important that people should be able to come to the Vigil than that the symbolism should be perfect. And so the Decree makes provision for fixing the time of the Vigil somewhat earlier wherever the bishops consider it necessary. So long as it is kept during the hours of darkness all that is absolutely essential in the symbolism is preserved.

To grasp this central idea inherent in the Vigil we must reflect that this, our Christian Pasch, has its origins in the Jewish Pasch which it has superseded. But precisely because it remains a pasch, it keeps some of the characteristics of its prototype, especially this feature of the night watch.

The Jews, ever since their original exodus from Egypt, spent this night in watching and prayer, clad in their traveling garments, with staves in their hands. They were ordered by Moses to celebrate the Pasch in this manner every year.

The first reason for it was to commemorate their liberation *in the past,* to bring back vividly to their minds the most important event in their history, namely, their constitution as the chosen people of God. So effective a means to this end was the paschal supper that it would have been justified on this ground alone.

But there was another and even more important purpose. There was a vital realism in their festival. They were not only remembering the past, but they were *waiting for the future.*

While recalling that God had passed among His people in days gone by, they were consciously waiting for God to pass among His people yet again. They were waiting for "Him who was to come"—their long-promised Messiah. Their liberation in bygone days pointed to another liberation which, they knew, might come any day whatever.

The religious ideals of the Jewish people were not centered on the past. They were anchored, indeed, in the past, but centered in the future. Theirs was a forward-looking religion. In the certainty which the past gave to them, they were always intent on the future, always waiting, always hoping, always desiring and longing for the coming of their Messiah.

And while this expectancy was with them habitual, they consciously exercised themselves in it and were pre-occupied with it when celebrating their Pasch. They always hoped that each Pasch would be not merely commemorative, but the real Pasch, the fulfilment, of which the ancient Pasch was only a figure or type.

Now this situation of the Jews as they celebrate their Pasch is exactly paralleled in us, the new chosen people, as we celebrate *our* Pasch.

For we, too, are *looking back* at a day of deliverance which we commemorate; we, too, are recalling how it is that we became a chosen people. If we did nothing but that, our vigil would still be worth while.

But it has a much deeper purpose. It is meant to make us *look forward*. For we, too, are waiting for something; we, too, are looking for another passage of the Lord among His people; we, too, are full of expectancy, longing for "Him who is to come." And we want Him to find us ready in mind and heart for the wonderful Exodus which His second coming will make possible.

Ours also is a forward-looking religion. Like the Jews, we are anchored in the past, but are intent on the future.

For the passover to which we look back—Christ's passover—has interest for us primarily because we know it is going to be followed by another passover of Christ *and also of ourselves* in the future. Christ will one day re-appear in glory at the Parousia. He will then claim us as His own, and will lead us to our promised land. We shall pass to God from this vale of tears, this exile, to rejoice for all eternity with Christ, the first-born among the sons of men.

So our Vigil is not just a remembering of the past; still less is it a kind of pious play-acting during which we pretend to be waiting for Christ to rise on Easter morning, as if he has not already risen two thousand years ago. Our Vigil is something very real; it is an *actual* waiting, an *actual* looking forward to and preparing for the Parousia. We are consciously and of set purpose doing on this one night of the year that which we *ought* to be doing in spirit throughout the whole of our lives—waiting for the coming of Christ.

This longing for the Parousia is an essential element in the true Christian outlook, for it figures so largely in the teaching of the Apostles. We find it in the epistles of St. Peter, St. John and St. Jude; the epistles of St. Paul are just full of it; and the entire book of the Apocalypse is concerned with nothing else.

That the longing for the Parousia has become so enfeebled or even non-existent in the minds of modern Catholics is deplorable. The common attitude towards the Last Day is one of fear and trembling; it is thought of only under its aspect of a Day of Wrath and of Judgment when Christ will say to the wicked: "Depart ye cursed into everlasting fire."

But we who are His brethren, we who have been redeemed and incorporated into His Mystical Body, we who are the chosen people of the New and Eternal Testament ought rather to dwell on those other words which He will address to us: "Come ye blessed of my Father, possess ye the kingdom prepared for you."

If we truly love our Master we shall long for Him to come to us. There should be often in our hearts and even on our lips the prayer so typical of the early Christians: "Maranatha! Come, Lord Jesus!"

One of the most valuable effects of the restored paschal Vigil, provided it be properly explained, is likely to be the restoration to Catholics of our own day of this important element in the true Christian outlook—the longing for the Parousia. Watching and waiting throughout the night will teach us, by the solemnity of the proceedings, to put ourselves into those dispositions which, alas, are so seldom recalled to us these days, though they loomed so large in the minds of early Christians. They were not content with one vigil per year; for generations they had one every week, to usher in their weekly celebration of the redemptive Mysteries.

We cannot rise to those heights; but thanks to our Holy Father Pope Pius XII, we have again at least *one* annual occasion on which the whole Church can reassemble to watch and wait; on this holy night the Church can do as a whole, consciously and explicitly, that which she does in spirit at all times; she can fulfil visibly the duty of the Spouse awaiting the coming of the Bridegroom for the eternal nuptials.

Passion Sunday

THE CONTENT OF THE VIGIL

It is in the spirit of expectation, of longing for the Parousia, that we are to celebrate our paschal Vigil. In this final instruction before Holy Week begins, let us briefly review the things we shall then do together.

On Palm Sunday we shall acclaim Christ, our King, as He comes to do battle for us, conquering the powers of evil by the glorious weapon of His Cross; and we pledge ourselves to follow Him in spirit, living over again with His Church the fateful events of His passage from this world to His heavenly glory.

On Maundy Thursday we are reminded of His great love for us; that love which prompted Him to dedicate Himself to death for our sakes, and to leave us a sacramental memorial so wonderful that, by its means, we would ever be able to make that death present to ourselves, to show it forth until He comes.

On Good Friday we shall contemplate the suffering which He bore for love of us, and venerate the Cross on which He died; then we are privileged to unite ourselves sacramentally, in Holy Communion, with the very Victim of the Cross.

On Holy Saturday we shall pass the day without celebrating the Eucharist, uniting ourselves in spirit with the Church who, as the Spouse of Christ, mourns because her Bridegroom has been taken away. And then on Saturday night we assemble to rejoice in His victory by celebrating the paschal Mysteries.

We come together elated in the thought that our salvation has been wrought. The first thing that meets our gaze as we arrive at the church is a fire burning outside it. It is a new fire, just enkindled by sparks struck from a flint or rock. We remember how Christ came forth from the rock which was His tomb; we remember that He said He had come to cast fire on earth, a fire which He ardently desired to enkindle. It is the fire of God's love which should burn in our hearts.

The celebrant takes a great candle, and inscribes on it Alpha and Omega—the first and last letters of the Greek alphabet. Christ is the beginning and the end—the beginning of our salvation when He came for the first time, and the end of it when He will come for the second time.

The priest implants into the candle five grains of incense—of incense which symbolizes worship. They remind us of the five worshipful wounds of Christ, and make us see in this candle a representation of Christ Himself. The candle is lighted and becomes even more Christlike—for Christ was the Light of the World. *"Lumen Christi,"* "The Light of Christ," sings the deacon. *"Deo gratias,"* we reply, greeting this Light which shines in the darkness.

We enter the church, led by the pillar of fire as the Israelites were led by a pillar of fire on the night of their liberation. Christ was the "light of men," and we now see this light communicated to men who are near it, just as Christ first spread His light to His apostles and disciples.

But these in turn have spread the light to countless other men, even to ourselves who live so long after them. And so the light is spread again from those who first received it from the great Christ-candle, to all the rest of us who are celebrating our salvation.

And now the deacon sings to us the paschal proclamation. He proclaims to us the glory of this night in a song of unsurpassable beauty, the *Exsultet*. We are to rejoice, he tells us, in the triumph of the mighty King, for He has wrought our salvation. "This is the Easter feast in which the true Lamb was slain . . . the night which scatters the darkness of sin . . . which restores to grace all who believe in Christ . . . for it is the night wherein Christ burst the bonds of death and came forth as a conqueror from the grave."

Next we listen, in the Scripture readings, to the story of God's preparations for our redemption. We hear about the original creation which foreshadowed that new creation that Christ has effected in us; we are reminded of the Passover of the Jews, of the prophecies concerning the Savior who, in those days, was still to come that He might make us into a new chosen people, to be led by Him into a new promised land.

But the Jews were constituted into a people only by passing through the waters of the Red Sea. Our constitution as a people took place in a similar manner—we all passed through waters of Baptism. The wonder of our Baptism is among the chief lessons we have to learn this night. So we sing the Litany of the Saints, begging the help of those who, as the result of passing through these waters, have actually entered into the promised land of heaven; and while doing so we watch the preparations in the sanctuary for the blessing of baptismal water.

This blessing is done with many instructive prayers and ceremonies; chief among them are the breathing on the water which indicates the action of the Holy Spirit, the lowering into the water of the paschal Candle representing Christ, and the pouring in of the Sacred Oils in the name of the Holy Trinity.

If there are any candidates for Baptism, this is the moment when that sacrament will be conferred upon them. But in any case there will take place the public renewal of baptismal vows by all.

Now this is of very great importance; if we enter into it whole-heartedly, it can make on us a deep impression that will go far to supply something that most of us lack, namely, baptismal-consciousness.

A convert, baptized in adult life, goes through a tremendous experience; he realizes what is involved; he is deliberately turning his back on his former life, changing his whole out-look, tearing himself loose from many ties, embracing new ideals and new obligations in a totally new environment. His Baptism is a conclusion, a prize finally achieved, as the result of strivings and hardships and a complete revolution in his own mind. He experiences a breaking with the past and an embracing of the future which shakes him to the core.

But most of us lack any such profound experience, for we were baptized as infants. We just grew up in our faith as a matter of course; we became accustomed to the fact that we were baptized Catholics without adverting to all that this means.

Yet we *ought* to realize it; we *ought* to be conscious of it; we need something to impress it powerfully upon us. And in the renewal of vows at the Easter Vigil we have what we need.

We hold in our hands the lighted Christ-candle; we answer the questions not in the singular, but in the plural—that is, not as individuals but as a body. This should bring home to us that in Baptism we became members of the Mystical Body of Christ. "We are Christ's Body, members of it, depending on one another" (1 Cor. 12:27). The share in the Christ-life which is ours did not come to us in isolation; we have it only because we are incorporated into the grace-filled Body which is the Church. We must know that to live the grace-life means to live the Church's life.

By pronouncing the baptismal vows we express our deliberate adherence to Christ. We make a solemn pledge that we turn from the evil and embrace good; we die to sin that we may live to Christ. We are buried with Him that we may rise with Him to newness of life. For in our Baptism Christ rescued us from the kingdom of darkness and transformed us into His own kingdom of light.

We must live, then, as children of the light. We must be heavenly-minded, not earthly-minded. "Risen now with Christ we must lift our thoughts above, where Christ sits at the right hand of God" (Col. 3:1). All that is what we pledge when we renew our vows.

By consciously adhering to Christ we cling to Him in whom alone there is salvation. For He has already passed over from this world; He died, but He rose again and ascended to heaven. By Baptism we have died and risen in Him spiritually.

We have yet to die and rise physically, but even now we have utter certainty that this will one day happen to us all. But will our physical rising from the dead be followed by an ascension into heaven with Christ? That is not certain. That all depends on whether we remain faithful to Him.

The day will inevitably come when we die in Adam—the first Adam. If then we are alive in Christ, the second Adam, we shall share His victory; otherwise not. When He comes at the Parousia He will claim only those who are His. Only those who are still "in Him" will ascend with Him.

It is for us, then, by fidelity to our baptismal vows, to ensure that we belong to Him on that great day, and that to us He will speak the welcome words, "Come ye blessed of My Father, possess ye the kingdom prepared for you."

We, the baptized, look forward to the second coming of Christ. We who stand with lighted candles in our hands, long for the coming of the Bridegroom.

Shall we in fact rejoice in the Parousia next Holy Saturday night? Who knows? It is possible at any time. But this much is certain: if Christ does not come to us then at the end of history, we may be sure that He will come to us in the course of Mystery. For we shall bring our celebration to its fitting close in the sacramental renewal of the Passover.

We shall do what He commanded us to do at His own Passover. We shall take bread and wine; we shall eat the Bread and drink the Cup to show forth the death of the Lord until He comes. And that very night He will come; the Lord will again pass among His people; He will come into our very hearts as we all share in the sacrificial banquet which is the Pasch of old made mysteriously present in our Easter Mass.

But it will be more than a memory of the past; more even than the making present of the past. It will be also the *pignus vitae futurae*—the pledge of eternal life. For we shall be eating of that Bread, of which if a man eat, he shall live forever. "If any man eat of this bread," said our Lord and Master, "I will raise him up on the last day."

And thus our Easter Communion is a sacramental conclusion in which the Parousia is anticipated, is made present in advance, giving to the chosen people of Christ a foretaste of the eternal passover to come.

Let me conclude by exhorting you all very earnestly to take part with fidelity and diligence in the Holy Week services. Put aside all other affairs during this great week, and attend every single service.

If it is truly impossible that you should come to all of them—if you cannot help missing something—at least let it not be the paschal Vigil. At all costs you should take part in that, for it is, in a very special way, the liturgical celebration in which you yourselves, in collaboration with Christ in His Church, work out in your own souls the subjective redemption which He wrought for you objectively so long ago.

PART TWO

Chapter One

OF PALM SUNDAY

Holy Week opens on Palm Sunday morning with a ceremony that can be most impressive and dramatic if conditions are such that it can be carried out realistically. It all began in Jerusalem where, very long ago, there grew up a custom of acting over again the triumphant entry of our Lord into that city, over the very path which He followed. The people assembled in a chapel near Bethany, the place from which our Lord started; and they accompanied the Bishop (who represented Christ) singing psalms of praise, shouting Hosannas, and waving the branches of palms and olives. This practice spread throughout the Christian world, and became formalized.

What really matters in all this is the procession of the people from some place representing Bethany to some other place representing Jerusalem. In those Catholic parts of Europe where processions through the streets are feasible, the normal thing is for the people to assemble in some chapel other than the parish church. This stands for Bethany. Palms are blessed and distributed there; and afterwards all go in procession, singing and waving their palms, to the parish church which stands for Jerusalem.

Since the Middle Ages the Palm Sunday service tended to

obscure its main point—the procession. The emphasis came to be put on the blessing of the palms, and an elaborate rite grew up about them which looked rather like a Mass before the Mass; it had an Introit, Collect, Epistle, Gospel, Preface and many long prayers. By contrast the procession became a mere token, done just by the clergy and a few servers.

But now, in its restored form, the Palm Sunday service is full of meaning. I suppose we shall continue to call it "Palm Sunday" through force of habit, but it has another name, "The Second Sunday of Passiontide." We should think of it as the day on which we are publicly to manifest our loyalty to Christ our triumphant King as He goes to do battle for our sakes. We are to accompany Him in spirit through His bitter Passion and Death and, as it were, to cheer Him on His way. As for the palms, they can be branches of yew trees or laurel or box or any local shrub. They are blessed with a single prayer.

The new rite emphasizes the procession and the fact that the people themselves are to take part in it. The rubrics expressly say that they are to answer the responses and to sing during the procession. It ought, moreover, to be a long procession, outside the church, not just going round inside. If the parish school or other property is not too far from the church, it is a good idea for the people to meet there for the blessing and distribution of the branches. Then they can all come in procession to the Church, singing their hymns on the way. This makes the ceremony much more "real," and like the original occasion when the people accompanied Our Lord from Bethany to Jerusalem. This way of doing it is provided for in the rubrics. But if there really is no other place which can be used to represent Bethany, the next best idea would seem to be to have the blessing of the branches at a side altar in the church. Then, if the church has at least two doors, the procession of all the people (not merely the clergy) can go out through one door and return by the main door. At any rate they ought to go outside the church (unless this is quite impossible), and the route for the procession should be quite long. That is what the rubrics say.

(Explain now what is going to be done in *this* church; if there are insuperable difficulties against doing any of the above things, explain them!)

During the procession antiphons are sung which explain what it is all about. (Read one of them in translation.) The most important of the items to be sung is the hymn to Christ the King which starts *"Gloria laus et honor tibi sit."* It was composed by Bishop Theodulf of Orleans in the ninth century, and he wrote no less than thirty seven verses of it, after each of which the people used to sing the chorus. That shows what long processions they used to have in those days—they might even go a mile and last most of the morning! Now we have only a few verses of the hymn, but still the same chorus is repeated after each verse, and all the people should join in this chorus. And after that, if time permits, the people may sing other hymns in honour of Christ the King.

This procession takes us in spirit right back into the past. Yet it is more than a mere memory; for in our procession we are actually accompanying Christ *here and now*. How is that true? Because Christ is present in three ways; firstly in mere symbol, on the Cross which heads the procession; secondly, in His representative the priest; thirdly in all of us as a community gathered together in His name. We are the Church of this place; and Christ, according to His promise, is in the midst of us.

But also this procession looks to the *future*. Christ, in His redemptive work, passed from this world into heaven, which is called the New Jerusalem. If our church stands for the earthly Jerusalem of old, it stands also for the New Jerusalem of heaven. When Christ comes again at the end of the world, He will lead our risen bodies, now joined to their souls, into heaven.

And so, as we enter now with Christ's representative, the priest, we should think of the day when we hope to enter heaven itself with Christ our King. Our procession is a kind of rehearsal, in a symbolic way, of our final passover on the Last Day.

As this main door of the church represents the gate of heaven it is a good idea to have it decorated on Palm Sunday, with branches of palms or olives or other trees, or garlands of flowers as they do in some of the churches in Rome. Then it will be like one of those triumphal arches under which Roman Emperors used to pass when celebrating victory in battle. But who is so great a victor as Christ? Whoever won such a tremendous battle as he did? Let us decorate our church door for Him on the day when we acclaim Him as conqueror!

(Ask for volunteers to be responsible for the collection of materials and the work of decorating the door on the eve of Palm Sunday.)

Now let us turn our minds from the future to the past. Christ and His followers entered Jerusalem, just as we now enter this church. But why did He go to Jerusalem? Was it to be crowned there as King? Not at all. He went there to suffer and die for our sakes, and to win through all His terrible passion and death to His resurrection. Our salvation depends on following Him; we must die with Him if ever we are to rise with Him. And therefore in the official prayer of the Mass, which the priest lays before God as our spokesman, we ask that "with the lesson of His endurance before us, we may be found worthy to have fellowship in His resurrection." How earnestly we should add our *Amen* to that prayer.

Then we hear from St. Paul, in brief summary, the whole story of Christ's work for us. Though in the glory of heaven, He came down to earth, taking "the nature of a slave, fashioned in the likeness of men . . . He lowered His own dignity, accepted an obedience which brought Him to death, death on a cross. That is why God has raised Him up . . . and given Him a Name which is above all other names." "Every tongue must confess Jesus Christ as the Lord, in the glory of God the Father." That is a perfect summary of the whole course of events we are to celebrate during Holy Week. Part of this story took place in heaven, part on earth. So now we turn our minds to what happened on earth.

We have it in the Gospel of St. Matthew now read to us. We stand to listen with pity and gratitude to the history of the Passion. We hear about the Agony in the garden, the betrayal and all the terrible things which followed it until our Lord and Master was laid in His grave. But all the while we are to remind ourselves that this was no failure, no defeat; it was all deliberately done, that He might enter into His glory.

From the past we turn to the present. We celebrate the Mass; there, upon the altar of our parish church, Calvary is made mystically present. It is the perfect conclusion to our prayerful listening to the history of the Passion. With especial vividness "we call to our minds the blessed passion and death" of God's Son, while the palms that we so lately held will not let us forget "His resurrection from the grave and His glorious ascension into heaven."

And at the end of it all we take our palms home, and reverently place them behind our crucifix; and we would do well to use the palms of all the members of our family, placing them in the living room, the kitchen, the bedrooms, the garden—in any place where we pass our time—that they may remain there throughout the year.

Why should we do that? Because at the end of the procession the priest says this prayer: "Lord Jesus Christ, our King and Redeemer, we have carried these branches and sung solemn praises in Thy honor. Graciously let Thy grace and blessing rest wherever these branches are brought; with the power of Thy right hand defeat every evil influence and deception of the devil while granting Thy protection to those whom Thou hast redeemed; who are living and reigning with God the Father in the unity of the Holy Spirit, one God for ever and ever. Amen."

The palms are not instruments of magic; they are not like superstitious amulets supposed to possess any power or virtue of their own; but they are the visible signs of the powerful prayer of God's Church which calls down the blessing of God upon all the places where they are put. We who have faith in the Church should have faith in her prayers, and make use of their power to our sanctification and protection.

(The instruction might well end with a singing lesson. Teach them *Gloria laus,* that they may be able to join in the chorus; it has but two lines, and those not specially difficult. They might also be taught the *Pueri Hebraeorum,* which could be sung by all after each choir verse if the branches are going to be distributed. This is no longer of obligation, since the people may hold the branches in their hands during the blessing; but it is surely desirable at least in small churches where the distribution would not take very long, and in any case for those in the sanctuary. The *Pueri Hebraeorum* could also be used in the procession after the *Gloria laus,* for it certainly ranks as a hymn in honour of Christ the King. Admittedly those present at these instructions would form only a part of the congregations attending the actual services; but they could give a lead to the others who might pick up the tunes from them.)

Chapter Two

OF HOLY THURSDAY

The Holy Week services all lead up to the Easter Vigil. The next one to consider, after Palm Sunday, is the ceremony of Holy Thursday. Its official title is *Feria Quinta in Cena Domini,* which means "The Thursday of the Lord's Supper." That title indicates to us the dispositions in which we should take part in it. We are to think of ourselves, even feel ourselves, as disciples in the Upper Room gathered about our Lord for a fraternal meal.

The Mass of Maundy Thursday, then, is in a special way a Mass of Christian unity, for it commemorates the Last Supper. On this night our Lord explicitly dedicated Himself to that death of the morrow whereby He would unite man with God. He gave to His apostles a moving and earnest discourse about their unity. He prayed to His heavenly Father, "Father, keep them true to Thy name, that they may be one, as we are one." He gave them an example of mutual charity by washing their feet; He gave them His own special commandment—that they should have love for one another. He gave them the Sacrament of love and of unity—the Blessed Sacrament; and He ended with the teaching which best shows the perfection of their unity with Him and with each other, telling them:

"I am the Vine, you are the branches." The quintessence of the Maundy Thursday spirit, then, is the spirit of unity.

The Church embodies this spirit both in her liturgy and in her legislation about it. On this day there should be only one Mass in each church, so that all the faithful should be gathered together in unity to partake of the one sacred banquet, instead of coming to various Masses at different times. Even priests are not allowed to celebrate, each one his personal Mass, at different altars; all must gather with their brethren at the one altar to share in the one Sacrifice by receiving from the hand of the Pastor that Bread that makes us all one.

However, when there are special circumstances to warrant it, the bishop may allow an extra Mass on Holy Thursday; but this, too, must always be in the evening, like the principal "Mass of the Last Supper," and it may never be a private Mass.

The spirit of the Last Supper receives expression in a ceremony, officially called the *Mandatum,* which may now be included in the Mass of the Last Supper, after the reading of the Gospel. The name Maundy is an old English form of the Latin word *Mandatum. Mandatum* means "Commandment" and comes from the phrase our Lord used just after He had washed the feet of His Apostles: "A new commandment I give unto you, that you have love for one another."

And now I want to draw your special attention to a Maundy Thursday ceremony of unity which you will not see. It is still in the books, though it is never used now. I refer to the Reconciliation of Penitents. In the ancient days of public penance, it was on this morning that absolution was given to those who, by reason of their sins, had been excluded from holy Communion. They were again made one body with their brethren, that they might share on this day in the banquet of unity.

Though we no longer use this ceremony, we ought certainly to keep its spirit. We should realize that the right time to receive absolution is in a Confession made *before* Maundy

Thursday, not after it. There are many, alas, who defer their Easter Confession till Holy Saturday, with the result that priests are inundated with crowds on the night of the holy Vigil itself. The instructions which were issued by order of the Pope concerning the restored Holy Week indicate that this is to be discouraged; not only does it lead to manifest inconveniences, but it is contrary to the spirit of the liturgy. People should make their Confessions in time for that Feast of Unity which is the Maundy Thursday Mass.

No doubt it will take years to educate the people at large out of the bad habit of waiting till Holy Saturday for their Confession; but at least you good people who are showing enough interest in the proper celebration of Holy Week to attend these instructions will surely take this to heart. Make sure that your Confession is on the Wednesday of Holy Week at latest.

The Mass of Maundy Thursday is a blend of joy and of sadness. There is joy because the Church celebrates the institution of the Mass, and the stupendous gift of the Body and Blood of Christ which was entrusted to her that night. There is joy especially for priests, for it was on this night that our Lord first shared His priesthood with men, giving to the apostles the command and the power to do what He had done. For these reasons the altar is adorned with flowers, white vestments are worn, and the *Gloria* is sung, to the accompaniment of the ringing of bells and the exultant pealing of the organ.

But there is also sadness, for this was a "farewell meal" that our Lord was eating with His disciples. Moreover there was cast over it the terrible shadow of the treachery of Judas. The Church is, as it were, haunted with this thought and keeps on bringing it up again and again. We find it in the Office of Matins which prepares for the Maundy Thursday Mass; the collect of the Mass makes mention of it; even the

Canon of the Mass is changed to bring this thought in.

There is a play on the Latin word *traditio,* which means a "handing over." Our Lord was "handed over" in treachery by Judas; St. Paul in the Epistle says that he is "handing on" the story of the Last Supper as he received it; the Canon prayers say that Christ "handed over" to His disciples the sacramental rite of His Body and Blood for them to celebrate. With special reverence and gratitude, therefore, we should receive that sacred Body and Blood on Holy Thursday when They are "handed over" to us by the priest in Communion. On this day, when we commemorate Christ's gift of Himself *for* us (through the treachery of Judas) and His gift of Himself *to* us (in the institution of the holy Eucharist) we should give ourselves to Him with an earnestness and sincerity unsurpassed on any occasion in the whole year.

It is by receiving Holy Communion that the people most closely share in the sacrifice of the Mass, for they are eating together of the Sacred Victim which has been offered to God. This is true, even when they are given hosts from a ciborium which has been consecrated at some previous Mass and kept in the tabernacle, because all Masses are Calvary made present again, and any consecrated host is the Victim of Calvary Who is offered at every Mass. And yet there is something lacking in the perfection of the symbolism, for the Mass at which these hosts from the tabernacle were consecrated is not the same liturgical act as that in which the people are now taking part. It was a Mass offered, perhaps by some other priest, on a different day, with different people. The symbolism is more perfect, and the sharing in the Mass is more immediate if the people are given hosts which "have been consecrated at that same Mass which they themselves have helped to offer," as the Pope says in the encyclical *Mediator Dei.* This is an ideal which cannot always be carried out in practice; but the Pope says that "the Church encourages it and wishes that it be not omitted." On this one day in the year the Church will not allow that it be omitted; it is now prescribed that at the Maundy Thursday Mass the people are in fact to be given "hosts consecrated at that same Mass which they themselves have helped to offer." For this reason the tabernacle is to be emptied before Mass begins, and the ciboria containing the altar-breads for Communion on this day and the next day are placed upon the altar. Communion from the tabernacle is thus forbidden; it must be Communion from the altar, so that everyone may share in the fullest possible sense in the very Mass they are helping to offer.

And so we have another striking manifestation of that Christian unity which is the feature of the "Mass of the Last Supper"; for priest and people all eat together of the very Victim which they have offered together. Moreover the *Confiteor* and other prayers which usually separate the Communion of the priest from that of the people have been cut out on this day. No sooner has the priest taken his share of the sacrifice than he turns at once to give their share to those who have offered it with him and through him.

After the distribution of Communion there will be left in the ciboria enough hosts for the Communion of the priest and people next day; so at the end of the Mass they are taken in procession to the Altar of Repose. Until the fourteenth century the Blessed Sacrament was merely taken away unostentatiously by the deacon at the end of Mass, and was locked up in the sacristy or other convenient place, without any external signs of honor. But the spread of devotion to the Blessed Sacrament as the abiding presence of Christ amongst us had been steadily growing since the establishment of the Feast of *Corpus Christi* a century earlier. The procession with lights and song which is the feature of *Corpus Christi* made people feel that there ought to be lights and song when the Sacred Host is moved from one place to another on Maundy Thursdays. So gradually this custom grew up, and by the fifteenth century it was quite general.

During the procession there is sung the beautiful hymn *Pange lingua* composed by St. Thomas Aquinas. Meditate especially on the third verse, of which this is a translation:

> On the night of that last supper,
> Seated with His chosen band
> He, the paschal victim eating,
> First fulfils the law's command,
> Then, as food to all His brethren
> Gives Himself with His own hand.

You are all thoroughly familiar with the verses *Tantum ergo sacramentum* and *Genitori Genitoque* which are sung at Benediction. Did you know that they are the last two verses of this Maundy Thursday hymn? The practice of paying visits to the Altar of Repose, and of "watching" with Christ during the night is thus a legacy of medieval piety—a precious one, too, which we must preserve and foster in every possible way.

It is worth referring also to another Maundy Thursday ceremony which you will not see, unless you are able to go to a Cathedral for it. Because this one takes place only in Cathedrals, and at the Mass celebrated by the Bishop. It is the consecration of the Holy Oils during a special Mass in the morning.

There are three oils which the Church uses in her sacraments and more solemn blessings; they are the Oil of Catechumens, the Oil of the Sick, and Holy Chrism. Oil of Catechumens is used in Baptism, in Holy Orders and at the blessing of fonts and altars. Oil of the Sick is used for Extreme Unction and also, curiously enough, in the consecration of church bells. Why for bells? They are not sick! No—but their sound can reach and comfort the sick who are unable to come to church, and by stimulating them to prayer in union with those who go to worship when the bells ring, their very sound can contribute to the sanctification of sick people. Holy Chrism is the most important of these three oils; it is regarded as the vehicle of the Holy Ghost's action, and is used in Baptism, Confirmation, the Consecration of bishops, of churches, altars, chalices, patens, fonts, and also of bells.

These oils are themselves consecrated by the Bishop at various points of the "Mass of the Chrism" in a solemn and picturesque ceremony. All sacraments impart to us the fruits of the redemption; that is why the oils needed for the administration of certain sacraments are consecrated during that week when the redemption is celebrated. Only the Bishop has the power to do this.

Here we have a reminder of the fact that the Church really is built "on the foundation stones of the apostles" who were the first bishops. The Church as a whole is made up of the flocks of the various bishops; and each flock receives all the means of sanctification from its bishop. The priests are but his assistants; they draw all their powers from him; they offer Mass and administer sacraments only as his representatives. Every altar is but an extension of the bishop's altar; every font is but a localization of the Cathedral font; every church is but an annex of the Cathedral. All these are consecrated by the bishop, or with oils that are blessed by him and impress on them as it were, the sanctifying power which he alone possesses to the full. Every priest is ordained by the bishop; every person is confirmed by him; and though not all are baptized, absolved or anointed by the bishop in person, they can only receive these sacraments from a priest who has "faculties"—that is, permission to use his priestly powers—from the bishop. And the oils used in blessing fonts, in baptizing and in anointing the sick are oils blessed by the bishop on Maundy Thursday.

Thus the diocese as a whole is really one Church; there have to be many buildings and many different assemblies (that is, congregations) because of great numbers and distances. But fundamentally all these are one; they are the Bishop's Church, he is their true Pastor; it is he who sanctifies them.

At least once in your lifetime you ought certainly to make the effort to go to your Cathedral on Maundy Thursday morning to witness the consecration of the Holy Oils. This interesting and impressive ceremony, in which the bishop is assisted by twelve priests, seven deacons and seven sub-deacons, will help you to realize the exalted position of the Bishop, and the unity of the whole diocese under him.

(Now by way of singing practice it would be well to go over again the *Gloria laus* and the *Hosanna,* and to make sure that the people know the *Pange lingua* for Maundy Thursday.)

Chapter Three

OF GOOD FRIDAY

The next of the Holy Week ceremonies which we have to consider in preparation for the paschal Vigil is that of Good Friday. It is absolutely unique—there is nothing of a like nature throughout the whole year. It has three parts of varying antiquity:

(a) A service of instruction and prayer.

(b) A service of Adoration of the Cross.

(c) A Communion service.

The first of these is the most ancient, and at one time was the only service held on Good Friday. The subject which occupies the Church on this day is the death of her Lord; and though it is impossible to divorce the Cross from the resurrection, it is the sense of mourning which predominates. The sanctuary is bare and unadorned; the altar is stripped, the candles are unlighted, only the crucifix remains, and even that is veiled in black.

A question may arise in your minds as to why the crucifix is veiled on the very day when, above all, we should be able to contemplate it. The answer is very interesting. In the early Church there were no such things as crucifixes, and the Cross was thought of, not as a gibbet of shame and torture, but as the glorious instrument of Christ's triumph. Crosses were made of the most precious woods, and adorned with jewels and gold. Later on, indeed, the figure of Christ was portrayed upon the Cross—but never as the mangled, suffering victim—always as the victorious King who reigned from the Cross. He was portrayed erect, clad in royal garments, with glorified wounds and a golden crown, eyes open, and an aspect of majesty and power.

But somewhere about the eleventh or twelfth century there gradually developed a change in popular piety, and there grew up a more lively devotion to the Passion of Christ considered under its sorrowful aspect. People concentrated on the bitter sufferings of the Sacred Humanity, to awake in their hearts sentiments of sympathy, love and contrition.

Those who approached Holy Week with such dispositions found it incongruous that the crucifix represented as the throne of the Triumphant Christ should be set before their eyes in the churches. In consequence the crucifixes were veiled at this time of the year, so that they would not distract the minds of the people from their thoughts of Christ's sufferings. Later still the style of crucifixes changed in conformity with this attitude; and Christ began to be represented on His Cross as dying in anguish with the blood streaming from His wounds and a crown of thorns upon His head. This style of crucifix gradually displaced the other even on altars. But because the custom of veiling the crucifix at this time had now acquired the force of law, it was continued even though the reason for it no longer obtained.

Thus we are in the curious situation of not being able to see the image of our suffering Lord just at the time when it would be most helpful to do so! One could wish that the rubric about veiling crucifixes could be modified, and declared to apply only to that type of crucifix which represents Christ as triumphant; and moreover that this latter type—the triumphant crucifix—were brought back into use for the ceremony of the Adoration of the Cross on Good Friday. For this would restore full meaning to the practice of having it veiled during the first part of the service, and of unveiling it for veneration after the history of the Passion and the following prayers are over.

The *reading-service* begins with an extract from the Prophet Osee. We may regard this as a prophecy in *word* of the coming redemption. The second is from the Book of Exodus, and we can regard it as a prophecy in *action,* for it is the story of the Passover of the Jews, the supreme type of the redemption. The third is from St. John's Gospel; it is the story of the Passion—the very matter that we have come to commemorate. We should listen with the closest attention to this account of all that our Lord suffered so willingly for our sakes, remembering that each of us, by his sins, has been a contributory cause of it.

After instructions, there comes *prayer*—in fact, a series of prayers. These were at one time a constituent of every Mass, not merely of the Good Friday service; they came after the Gospel, the last of the Scripture readings, just as they do here. Even now after the Gospel (or after the Creed if that be inserted) the priest greets the people with *Dominus vobiscum* and then says *Oremus,* "Let us pray." But we no longer have any prayers there—we get on with the Offertory. If the great "Prayer of the Faithful," as it is called, is ever restored to public Masses, this is the point at which it will come. Many of us hope that it will be restored some day in a form suitable to modern needs.

At any rate we may be glad that it has been retained at least on Good Friday, for it is a prayer "for all sorts and conditions of men." On this day God's mercy knows no bounds. Our Lord prayed on His Cross, "Father, forgive them, for they know not what they do." In that spirit the Church now prays not only for her own members of every station, but also for heretics, schismatics, Jews and pagans. And the manner of these prayers is especially solemn and impressive.

Firstly the priest announces the intention. (Read a sample from the Good Friday service, in translation.) Then the deacon sings *Flectamus genua,* "Let us kneel down." There follows a short pause, a truly pregnant silence, during which each member of the congregation should pour out his heart to God in fervent prayer, but in his own way, for the intention proposed by the priest. In a sense this may be called "private prayer" because each makes his own prayer—it is individual. Yet at the same time it is a highly liturgical prayer, for it is far from being individualistic. It is done by each in virtue of that "deputation to worship" which follows from his possession of the baptismal character; it is done, moreover, at the command, or deputation, of the deacon who acts as an official of the hierarchic Church when he bids all to sink to their knees in prayer. In addition, it is not a self-centered prayer, each being concerned with his own needs; it is, instead, directed to all the world-embracing intentions which the Church has so much at heart, and which she confidently hopes will be granted through the passion and death of Christ.

After this intensely personal form of prayer the deacon gives another command, *Levate,* "Arise"; and all stand up for the public prayer of the Celebrant which expresses in a formal manner, in the name of the community, that which each member has been praying for. (Read out a sample.) To this everyone should reply with a heartfelt *Amen.*

Now comes the second, and quite the most moving part of the Good Friday service, namely, the *Adoration of the Cross.* It started in Jerusalem in the fourth century after the True Cross had been discovered by St. Helena. The bishop used to bring forth a relic of the True Cross in a gorgeous reliquary of gold and silver; he and his clergy, followed by all the faithful, advanced in procession to kiss the relic, saluting it with joy as the instrument of Christ's victory.

This custom spread throughout Christendom and became somewhat elaborated into the form which remains with us until this day. Because most churches had no relic of the True Cross, a crucifix bearing the regal figure of the Triumphant Christ was used instead.

What happens now is that a large Crucifix is carried in with solemnity from the sacristy by the deacon; two acolytes walk before him, and two others, with lighted candles, walk on each side of him. The Crucifix is covered with a purple veil. While all the people stand in respect, the celebrant and subdeacon come forward to meet the procession. Having received the Crucifix from the deacon, the celebrant with his ministers and two of the acolytes goes to the Epistle side of the altar and faces the people. He then proceeds to unveil the Crucifix in three stages, singing with his assistants the *Ecce lignum crucis* "Behold the wood of the Cross." All the faithful reply *Venite adoremus,* "Come, let us adore"—and sink to their knees.

After this the Crucifix is held by two acolytes with its foot resting on the ground in the centre, just in front of the altar. The two acolytes with candles kneel down facing it from either side. The celebrant and all the clergy come one by one to kiss the feet of the crucified Saviour, making three genuflections as they advance.

When everyone in the sanctuary has thus venerated the Cross, it is carried down to the altar rails by the acolytes, and the people come up one by one to kiss it, each making a single genuflection before they do so.

While this is taking place, the choir sings a collection of beautiful sentences taken mostly from the Old Testament. You should not fail to read them for yourselves when not engaged in going to or returning from the kissing of the

Cross. They are known as "The Reproaches" and we should consider them as coming from the mouth of our Savior addressed to His ungrateful people. (Read one or two samples in English.)

But we must never forget that the Cross led to the resurrection; that though others may view it as a gibbet of shame, it is actually the instrument of our Lord's triumph. As such it was always regarded by the Church during the early centuries. This ancient spirit is expressed in the hymn *Crux Fidelis* by the sixth century poet Venantius Fortunatus, which concludes the ceremony of the Adoration of the Cross.

> Faithful Cross! in grove or woodland
> Standeth not a nobler tree!
> None in foliage, none in blossom,
> None in fruit thy peer may be;
> Sweet the wood and sweet the iron,
> Sweet the Load that hung on thee!

After this the deacon goes to the altar of repose to bring back the Blessed Sacrament, while the choir sings one or more antiphons to give the people matter for meditation. The first antiphon has the well known words: "We adore Thee, O Christ and we bless Thee, because by Thy holy Cross Thou hast redeemed the world."

The third and final part of the Good Friday liturgy is the Communion Service. This has a long and very interesting history. In the early ages of the Church the Mass was not celebrated every day, but only on Sundays, big feasts, Ember days, and some of the days of Lent. But not infrequently, on days when there was no Mass, the faithful nevertheless met together for a divine service which consisted of prayers and readings from Holy Scripture, rather like the present Mass from the Kyrie to the Gospel, only longer. At the end of it, because there was no Mass, they just said the Our Father together, and received Holy Communion.

Gradually Mass became more frequent until there was Mass every day except on Good Friday which thus remained as the only Communion service of the year. The next stage was to put in the Veneration of the Cross between the prayer-and-reading service and the Communion service; and finally, somewhere about the eleventh century, various features were introduced into the Communion service which made it look more and more like a Mass—though it never actually became one because there was no Consecration. When it came to look like a Mass it was called "The Mass of the Presanctified," and it continued like that until 1955 when the Mass-like features were eliminated and it was restored to its genuine form of a Communion service.

Another curious thing about it is that though it began as a Communion service, it was for the people only, and not for the clergy. So the priest who distributed Communion was not himself allowed to receive it on Good Friday. By the twelfth century everyone, including the priest, communicated; by the sixteenth century no one *except* the priest was allowed to communicate—and so it remained until our own times. But at last the wheel has turned full circle, and we are back where it all began, with a simple Communion service which is neither disguised as a Mass, nor exclusive of anybody, but is for all, both priest and people together.

It is a suitable conclusion to our Good Friday liturgy. Throughout the whole of it we have tried to enter as fully as possible into the saving passion and death of our Lord; first of all with our minds in our attentive listening to the account of His sufferings; then with our wills in exercising the universal charity taught us by Christ, in that we prayed for "all sorts and conditions of men;" next, in our emotions, by our grateful adoration of His Cross; and finally by sacramental union with the very Victim of the Cross given to us in

Communion. And by thus entering, in fourfold manner, into His passion and death we find ourselves carried along towards the glory of His resurrection.

For the Christ whom we receive in Communion is, in fact, the Risen Christ. His sufferings are all of the past, even though present to us both in memory and in symbol. The fact is that He has risen again, and death has no dominion over Him. It is Christ our Pasch who is sacrificed—He has completed His Passover and is now living and reigning for ever.

Our thoughts go forward to that eternal Pasch described by St. John in the Apocalypse: "I saw," he says of his vision, "in the midst, where the throne was, a Lamb standing upright, yet slain as though in sacrifice . . . and I heard in my vision the voices of a multitude of angels, in thousands of thousands, crying aloud: Power and Godhead, wisdom and strength, honor and glory and blessing are His by right, the Lamb that was slain. And every creature in heaven and on earth I heard crying out together: Blessing and honor and glory and power, through endless ages, to Him who sits on the throne, and to the Lamb."

(For singing practice people could be taught the *Venite adoremus* with which they are to answer the *Ecce lignum:* and they should be practised in the *Pater noster* which they are to say, all together, with the priest.)

Chapter Four

OF FIRE AND LIGHT

Tonight we start our consideration of the paschal Vigil. Why we hold a Vigil at all will be explained to you at Mass in one of the future morning instructions, so I cannot go into that now, except to say that the idea of listening to holy Scripture and praying during the night goes back to the Jews, and the Church took over the practice.

Now when the Jews passed the night in reading and singing psalms, they needed some light to do it by; therefore they began by lighting lamps and blessing the light. That custom also was taken over by the Church, but has died out except for this one night of the year, the holy Vigil of Easter.

Because of the special occasion, a significance has become attached to this light; the great paschal Candle has become a symbol of Christ, the Light of the world, and it is surrounded by a profusion of ceremonies, of which the chief one is the singing of the song of praise known as the *Exsultet*. This forms the first part of the service—*a festival of light*—which we shall examine now.

Light is something very wonderful indeed; yet we are so accustomed to it that we take it for granted. It is well to reflect for a few moments that light is the very first of God's creatures; we are told in the Bible that God began the whole of creation by saying "Let there be light." Without light this world could not be the beautiful place that it is; nothing at all could grow, and there would be no warmth whatever. It is therefore most fitting that our celebration of God's New Creation in the order of grace should also begin with the making of light; and it is fitting that we should honour the light so made by special blessings and prayers.

To light a candle we need a flame or fire; and so outside the church *a fire is lit* by sparks struck from flint. This should make us think of God, because in Old Testament times He often chose fire as a sign of His presence. For example, we read in the Book of Exodus: "The Lord appeared to Moses in a flame of fire out of the midst of a bush." And later, at Mount Sinai, we read that "all the mountain was in smoke; for the Lord was come down upon it in fire."

That is our first example tonight of what we call a *symbol*. A symbol is something which can remind us of something else. There are scores of them in the liturgy. Often a thing is used precisely because it is symbolic; for instance, the Sign of the Cross. If that movement did not remind us of the Cross of Christ, it would not be made.

But other things are done because they are practical—for instance, striking a light. This would be done, whether it meant anything or not, for the simple reason that a light is needed.

However, when an action is done or a thing used in the liturgy, even for practical purposes, very often we can see some meaning in it. The symbolism is not intrinsic, as with the Sign of the Cross, but extrinsic. The thing has *become* a symbol because our minds work on it. Sometimes the Church has directed our minds to it by pointing out some meaning in the prayer she uses to accompany the action or to bless the thing. That is one of the ways in which the Church teaches us.

An example is the prayer for the *blessing of this new fire*.

It was struck from a flint or stone; and the Church prays: "O God, through Thy Son, the true cornerstone. . . ." This is a reference to Psalm 117 which says, "The stone which the builders rejected is become the head of the corner." It applies to Christ; for the Jews wanted to build up their nation, but refused to do so on Him. They rejected Him. So now there is a new chosen people—the Church—built up on Christ; He joins all the members into one as a cornerstone joins the other stones about it.

The prayer continues: "Hallow now for our use and profit this new fire struck from stone, and grant us through this Easter feast to be so inflamed with desire for heaven that we may attain with pure souls to the feast of everlasting brightness." That expresses the spirit of the Vigil we are beginning; we are to yearn for heaven.

The phrase, "struck from a stone," indicates another symbolic meaning; in fact, two of them. The spark, naturally, stands for Christ; but what about the stone?

The more obvious meaning is that it stands for the rocky tomb in which Christ was buried and from which He came forth on this holy night. But some early writers of the Church have remarked that the stone is in no way broken when the spark comes forth from it; and so they see in its emergence a likeness to the birth of our Lord who came forth from His Mother's womb without any violation of her virginity.

After the blessing of the fire the priest takes the great candle and *cuts a Cross* on it. At once we think of Christ. The priest makes it clear that the candle is indeed to represent Christ by saying: "Christ yesterday and today, the beginning and the end, the Alpha and the Omega." These are the first and last letters of the Greek alphabet; and Christ is in truth the beginning and the end of our salvation. He began it when He came for the first time, and He will end it when He comes for the second time.

Now the priest writes on the candle the figures indicating the *current year,* saying: "His are the seasons, His the ages, to Him be glory and dominion through ages eternal. Amen." These last words come from the Apocalypse wherein is revealed to us the reign of the Risen Christ through all ages. They should remind us that the secular year, measured by the time taken for the earth to go round the sun, is but an image of the Church's year during which she gravitates round the Sun of Justice, Christ the Light of the World.

Inserting the *five grains of incense* increases the likeness of this candle to Christ, for they are an obvious reminder of His five glorious wounds.

He *lights the candle* from the new fire, and *blesses* it; these are the finishing touches of the preparation of the candle for its function of being to us an eloquent symbol of our Risen Savior. As such it now becomes the focal point of our worship; it is, in our minds, personified; it becomes the triumphant Hero in whose honor we hold a *procession,* and whose saving deeds are extolled by the deacon in his *panegyric.*

In both procession and panegyric the idea of "Light" should stimulate our minds in two ways—an Old Testament way and a New Testament way. In the procession the column of light going ahead in the darkness should make us think of the column of fire that went ahead of the Jews at the first Passover. It led them through the waters of the Red Sea towards the promised land. That is Old Testament.

But this candle stands for Christ who has gone ahead of redeemed mankind at His own passover two thousand years ago; but He is even now leading His new chosen people through the waters of Baptism towards the new promised land of heaven. All that is New Testament. And the point to grasp is that we ourselves, in this very year that has been inscribed upon the candle, are marching along behind Christ towards heaven. What is happening now to us is even more wonderful than what happened to the Jews.

But there is another New Testament thought which the procession brings home to our minds—that of Christ the Light of the World. We salute Him as such by answering *Deo gratias* to the proclamation *Lumen Christi* by the deacon. The light is spread from the great Christ-candle firstly to the priest, then to his ministers and servers, and finally to all the people.

The idea of Christ as the Light of the World is very old and goes back even to the prophets. Isaias said that the people who walked in darkness would see a great light—and he meant the Messiah. In the New Testament Zachary welcomed Him as the Light, saying that He was the Orient—the One who rises in the east—to shine on those who sit in darkness and in the shadow of death. Simeon said that He was the Light that should give revelation to the Gentiles.

Our Lord Himself claimed the title in His words, "I am the Light of the world; he that followeth Me walketh not in darkness, but shall have the light of life" (John 8:12).

Of course everyone knows the beginning of St. John's Gospel which is read at the end of Mass: "In Him there was life, and that life was the light of men . . . the light shines in the darkness, a darkness that was not able to master it. He enlightens every man born into this world. He was the true light."

And because the light of Christ shines upon us, we are called by St. John "children of the light . . . we are not of the night, nor of the darkness." And so, says St. Paul, "Let us therefore cast off the works of darkness and put on the armor of light." St. Peter reminds us that we are a chosen generation, a kingly priesthood, a holy nation, whom Christ has called out of darkness into his marvelous light.

How vivid all these thoughts should be in our minds as we stand there in the church which, a few moments ago, was so dark, but is now radiant in the light of the candles which we, the children of light, are now holding.

(For singing lesson; let the people have books containing the text of the Paschal Vigil; THE MASSES OF HOLY WEEK AND THE EASTER VIGIL published by The Liturgical Press, Collegeville, is recommended. Teach everything which the people have to sing, as far as the beginning of the Litanies. They will know most of it already as it is very easy; so there will probably be time to repeat the *Venite adoremus* and *Crux fidelis* and *Pater noster* taught on the previous occasion.)

Chapter Five

OF THE SONG OF PRAISE

Tonight let us consider the *Exsultet,* which is the song of the deacon in praise of the paschal Candle and of the paschal night. Some people have misunderstood this as being a *blessing* of the candle; but it is not a blessing (that was done outside the church door); it is a panegyric, a proclamation of the victory of Christ who rose triumphantly from His tomb.

In early days the deacon used to make up this song in fresh form each year, even though its subject was always the same. But, as so often happens with functions that have to be repeated, there was gradually evolved an accepted text which became fixed.

It is not quite certain who wrote the exquisitely beautiful and poetic text that we now have; some have thought it was St. Augustine, but the majority of scholars attribute it to St. Ambrose. In any case it goes back certainly to the fourth century.

When its lovely melody breaks the stillness of the paschal night in the thronged church made brilliant by the multitude of candle flames, no one, unless his soul be utterly devoid of poetic feeling, can remain unmoved, and yet we are not meant to be merely passive, drinking it all in. Our minds should be active to understand the meaning and implication of the text, and our hearts should sing with gratitude for the great mercies of God which are described to us in such exquisite terms.

It would have been possible for the Church to proclaim them in a prosaic and factual manner, as she does in the Creed with the words: "Born of the Virgin Mary, suffered under Pontius Pilate, was crucified, died and was buried. He descended into hell, the third day He rose again from the dead. He ascended into heaven, sitteth at the right hand of God the Father; from thence He shall come to judge the living and the dead." For that, really is the subject of the deacon's song.

But this is not an occasion for a mere recital of facts. The Church knows that we are more than just intelligences; we are human beings gifted with imagination and with emotions; she desires to move our hearts and wills, to make us thrill with wonder, throb with gratitude, and exult with joy. She speaks to us in terms filled with lyric poetry, with all manner of scriptural allusions to evoke images, recall stirring events of the past, and stimulate our yearnings for the future. She uses metaphor, paradox, hyperbole and all the other arts of rhetoric.

For she sings tonight not of mere facts but of mysteries—of the Christian mysteries first enacted by Christ long ago, but ever renewed amongst us in our paschal celebrations.

There was formerly a very interesting custom which did not die out until the middle ages; perhaps somebody might revive it some day! The words and music of the *Exsultet* were written out, not in a book with pages to be turned, but on a long parchment roll, beautifully illuminated with ornamental capital letters shining with gold and scintillating with bright colors. As the deacon sang from it, he had to unroll it; and the part which he had used then hung down from the front of his lectern in the sight of the people. And so there were drawn on it, upside down to the deacon so as to appear the right way up to the people, various pictures corresponding with the parts being sung.

For example, when he was singing, "let trumpets sound the triumph of the mighty King," the people could see a picture of the trumpeters; when he sang of the "candle wrought by the labor of bees," they could see a picture of a honeycomb with bees working on it to make the wax. It must have been rather exciting!

But even now, and without any pictures except those which we form in our minds, the *Exsultet* is exciting. The setting is perfect: the whole church ablaze with light while darkness reigns outside; all the people standing with lighted candles in their hands; the deacon arrayed in the most splendid white dalmatic which the parish can afford; in front of him, dominating the whole scene, the great paschal candle with its Sign of the Cross, Alpha, Omega, the date, the grains of incense, surmounted by its glowing flame.

There is a moment of expectant stillness; then he begins, to one of the loveliest tunes ever composed, an inspiring appeal that all heaven and earth should rejoice.

(Read from the text, p. 133, making any comments that seem suitable. A few suggestions follow.)

"for He has wrought our salvation." Content of paschal Mysteries. Confer the *Benedictus,* on page 178.

"darkness has everywhere been overcome." Satan called by our Lord the Prince of darkness. Darkness means ignorance (Zachary—"those who live in darkness"); darkness means sin (St. Paul, *passim*).

"ring with loud song." Exhort to join in the singing.

"invisible Father." It is Christ who "shows us the Father." St. Philip's request, and Christ's answer. Confer Christmas preface.

"debt of Adam." In Adam we all die, in Christ we rise. St. Paul to the Romans; teaching on the Second Adam.

"This is the night." Oft-repeated phrase; realism of the liturgy in which the power of the redemption is ever present and active. Cf. *Mediator Dei*. The liturgy has a quasi-sacramental value and efficiency, in that it is the Church which is celebrating this night. This does more than merely arouse emotions and instruct minds; the very fact that we participate in the liturgy of the paschal feast brings to us the effects of the redemption. "The holiness of this night drives out wickedness, washes away guilt, restores innocence to the fallen and joy to the sorrowful."

"restores them to grace and makes them co-sharers with saints." Expatiate on the dignity of Christians; eternal destiny; hope and longing.

"O truly necessary sin of Adam." Startling phrase inspired by consideration that our restored condition is in many ways superior to that of Adam in primeval innocence. Confer prayer *Deus qui humanae* in Mass.

"solemn oblation of this candle." This offering of the Christ-symbol is being made within a "eucharistic" (praising and thanking) prayer very like that within which, at Mass, Christ Himself is offered; beginning with a preface and ending with a doxology.

"heaven is wedded to earth and God to man." Christ as the Bridegroom, the Church as His spouse. Salvation through the Church, by membership therein.

"May the Morning Star behold its flame." This Morning Star is Christ; this phrase expresses longing for the Parousia, and the hope that it may happen on this very night.

(For singing practice: go through all the parts which the people should sing on Holy Saturday night, including the *Alleluia* which occurs at two points in the Mass, and the *Ite*. As they will know most of this from the previous occasion it may well be possible also to teach them the proper *Kyrie* wherewith the Mass begins.)

Chapter Six

OF THE PROPHECIES

After the *Exsultet* which we studied last time, the next item in the paschal Vigil is the reading of the so-called "prophecies." Till the recent reform there were twelve of them; now there are only four. All the more reason why we should seek to derive from this fewer number the maximum of spiritual profit.

The original purpose of these prophecies was to remind the Christian community—but especially the catechumens who were about to be baptized—of the wonderful manner in which God had created the human race and then prepared it, after the Fall, for the coming of Christ.

Obviously we shall not, tonight, go through the text of each one, but I shall just indicate what they are about and make a few remarks on each.

The *first prophecy* gives us the story of Creation, and it keeps on reminding us, after each stage, that "God saw that it was good." But as it mentions almost at once the fact that "the spirit of God was stirring above the waters," our minds turn easily to Baptism in which we were created anew "from water and the Holy Spirit," in a manner which is even more wonderful than that of our first creation. If it was good that God once evoked natural life from the water, how much better is it that He has brought forth supernatural life from the water after the redemptive work of Christ.

When we hear of the earth and the sea and the sun and the stars and the birds and the fish and the animals that God created, let us be grateful to Him for all the works of nature. And when we hear that "God created man in His own image," we should reflect how privileged we are thus to resemble our Creator, and endeavor always to serve Him well.

At the end of this prophecy the priest invites us to pray. The deacon tells us to kneel down, and we pass some moments in private prayer about what we have heard. This pause for private prayer is now explicitly ordered in the rubrics; and only after it are we bidden to stand up for the public prayer which the priest, as spokesman of us all, offers to Almighty God.

The *second prophecy* is the story of the liberation of the children of Israel from the slavery of the Egyptians. They were led dry-shod by the pillar of fire through the waters; but the Egyptians who were pursuing them were all overwhelmed.

That was the first Pasch; obviously it turns our minds to our own liberation by Christ. It is by passing through the waters of Baptism that we attain to "that freedom wherewith Christ has made us free."

"Moses and the Israelites sang a song to the Lord"—a song of praise and thanksgiving. Part of it will be sung by the choir after the reading of the prophecy. As we listen to it we should have no difficulty in making its sentiments our own.

Again we have a few moments of private prayer, followed by the public prayer sung by the priest. This one is particularly apt and beautiful (read it out from the text, page 141).

The *third reading* is much more difficult to understand. It comes from the Prophet Isaias who predicts that "the Bud of the Lord" will come to bring joy to the "survivors of Israel," and that those who are in Jerusalem shall be called holy. "The Bud of the Lord" is a poetic way of saying "The Messiah," that is, Christ. The "survivors of Israel" must mean those who remained faithful to God, namely the apostles and the disciples who received Christ, in contrast with the rest of Israel which rejected Him. The phrase refers, then, to the primitive Church. And we know that "Jerusalem" means the Church.

So we can interpret this prophecy by saying: "Christ will come to the apostles and disciples and will bring them joy. And those who are in the Church shall be called holy." Obviously all that has come true; for we who have become members of the Church by Baptism have now the title of "God's holy people." That title is used of us in the Canon of every Mass.

There follows a song about God's Vineyard, planted with the choicest vines. That again is a symbol of the Church. We often speak of the Church as "the vineyard of the Lord," and we are all branches of Christ who said: "I am the Vine, you the branches."

In our moment of private prayer which comes after this song, we will surely ask the grace to be very fruitful. That is precisely what the priest asks for us in the public prayer which follows: "Grant them the strength to root out the tangle of briars and thorns, and to bring forth worthy fruit in abundance." With all our hearts we will sing *Amen* to this.

Now the *last prophecy*. Moses knew that he had not long to live, so he called the people together and gave them a solemn warning about the danger of being unfaithful to God's laws. That is a lesson for us too; even though we are now God's people as the result of our Baptism, we must not deceive ourselves into thinking that we shall automatically go to heaven because of that. We have to remain faithful to God while we are wandering through the desert of this life; we must remain true to our baptismal vows. In a few minutes we shall have the opportunity of renewing these—so let us do it very earnestly.

This instructional service concludes with a prayer that God will help us always to be faithful.

Next, in preparation for the baptismal ceremonies which are to come, we ask by means of a *Litany* the prayers of all those who have been outstandingly faithful to God—the angels and saints in heaven. Those saints are our brethren; like us, they were baptized into the new chosen people of God; they have finished their wandering through the desert, and their souls have reached the promised land. They join with us on this holy night in looking forward to the Parousia, the second coming of Christ when we shall all have our bodies again, glorified after resurrection, like the glorified Body of our Savior; and with Him we shall all have our final passover into the land of eternal happiness.

We appeal first to God Himself for His mercy—to God the Father who created us, to God the Son who redeemed us, and to God the Holy Ghost who sanctifies us. Then we turn to Christ's holy Mother who is Queen of all the angels and saints. After her come the three great archangels; St. Michael who vanquished Lucifer; St. Gabriel who announced the Incarnation; and St. Raphael who accompanied Tobias on his journey. May he accompany us too on our journey through the perils of this life.

Now we turn to St. John the Baptist, St. Joseph and all the holy ones of the old dispensation, saved by their faith in the redemption still to be wrought; then come St. Peter and all the apostles and saints.

This Litany is very old indeed; scholars think it has come down to us from the third century, though, of course, the names of a few of the saints have been added to it since it was first sung.

It would be good for us to know at least one small fact that touches our imagination, concerning each one of the saints invoked; that makes the Litany very interesting and helps to keep our minds on it. In any case, remember that all these saints began their Christian lives as we did—by Baptism; and we have the same Mass and the same sacraments as they did, to help us towards heaven. Really there is no reason, except our own weakness, why we should not become as holy as they did. We are all called to holiness. So we can ask their prayers with confidence.

(For singing practice, repeat the *Kyrie* from last week, and concentrate on the *Gloria* which is more difficult. Perhaps also go once through the *Sanctus* that it may be easier to learn properly next week. Pp. 184 ff.)

Chapter Seven

OF BAPTISM

After the Litany come the *ceremonies pertaining to Baptism*. These are the blessing of the baptismal font, the administration of Baptism if any are to be baptized, and the renewal of baptismal vows.

Before we examine the liturgy, let us think for a little about Baptism. It has a twofold aspect, individual and social. It is individual because it has an effect on each person and is for his own good. But it is social because its effects are such as to relate that person to others, forming a society or community. It is an enrichment, therefore, of the community as well as of the individual.

For the individual, Baptism is a "new birth." As our Lord said to Nicodemus, "Unless a man be born again of water and of the Holy Ghost, he cannot see the kingdom of God." Birth is the beginning of life; this new birth of Baptism is thus the beginning of a new life—of supernatural life—for the individual. It is from the womb of his mother that a man is born into this life; and so the font, from which he is born into the new life, is called the womb of Mother Church.

Moreover, for the individual Baptism is a dying and a rising with Christ. The death and resurrection of Christ are paschal

Mysteries; they are the very things that we celebrate at the Pasch since it was by them that Christ Himself achieved His passover or passage from this world to His Father. If Baptism, then, is a sharing in the death and resurrection of Christ, there could be no more suitable time for its administration than at the celebration of the Pasch.

Again, Baptism is for the individual an enlightening by Christ. The light of Christ is thereby shed into his soul. "Once you were all darkness," wrote St. Paul to the Ephesians; "now, in the Lord, you are all daylight." The baptized can see with the eyes of faith, in the light radiated by Christ, many truths which are hidden from those who are not illuminated.

But if we look at Baptism only from the point of view of the individual we are missing an aspect which is absolutely fundamental. For it was instituted by our Lord as a sacrament of initiation—that is, a sacrament which makes us members of His Church. We are not saved as individuals; we are saved because we become members of Christ's Mystical Body which, precisely because it is His Body, is destined to share the triumph of its Head.

We learn this from its types in the Old Testament. It is the fulfilment of circumcision, the rite of initiation into the chosen people of old. St. Paul has a very striking passage on this point. "In Christ," he wrote to the Colossians, "you have been circumcised with a circumcision that was not man's handiwork . . . you, by Baptism, have been united with His burial, united, too, with His resurrection . . . He gave life to you when you were dead in your sins, with all nature uncircumcised in you" (Col. 1:10-13).

The early writers of the Church loved to point out the parallel that both rites—Circumcision and Baptism, are proper to "the eighth day." For circumcision was ordered by God to be given on the eighth day; and Baptism is a sharing in the resurrection of Christ which took place on the day after the

Sabbath. As the Sabbath is "the seventh day," that means that the resurrection was on "the eighth day." St. Cyril of Jerusalem, instructing his catechumens, even said that "we are circumcised in the Holy Spirit." Clearly its social effect is fundamental—it aggregates a man into the new chosen people.

The same point emerges from considering it as the fulfilment of the passage through the Red Sea. That was the ancient passover, in consequence of which the children of Israel were constituted into the chosen people. And now, at the new passover, men pass through the waters of Baptism and thereby become aggregated into the new chosen people. It is only as members of this chosen people that we shall be led into the promised land of heaven.

It is true, indeed, that Baptism is now given at any time; but it is pre-eminently a paschal sacrament, and Easter is the supremely fitting time for it. Even now the usual day for it is Sunday; and that is very right and proper since every Sunday is a "little Easter."

The clearest proof that Baptism is a sacrament of initiation is its indication as such by our Lord when He said to His apostles: "Make disciples of all nations, baptizing them in the Name of the Father and of the Son and of the Holy Ghost." And remember what Christ had taught about His Church—that it would be like a net containing fish, a sheepfold, a city—all of which things are collective.

Again, by Baptism we become adopted sons of God; that means that we are brethren of Christ our Lord and brothers and sisters of each other. We form one great family in Christ, and are referred to in these terms in many prayers of the Mass. Now the birth of a baby in the natural order is doubtless very important for the baby, but it is not merely the personal affair of the baby. The one who has most joy in this event is the mother; and it closely concerns all the other sons and daughters who have already been born.

In like manner the new birth of Baptism is important for the person baptized; but is far from being his affair alone. It brings joy to Holy Mother Church, and should be an event for all the other children of the Church, especially those of the local Church, that is the congregation of that particular place.

That is why the ideal setting for Baptism is at a meeting of the community which forms that local Church; public Baptism, at which Mother Church brings forth a new child, and at which those already begotten by the Church receive a new member into the family, gives the truest picture of what it all means. This ideal is realized at the paschal Vigil when there are any to be baptized.

In the restored paschal Vigil we have an opportunity of realizing the social importance of Baptism even if nobody be then baptized. For we have been given something quite new— a genuine liturgical innovation—in the form of the public renewal of baptismal vows.

Often it has been stressed that the liturgy should not be just an affair of the clergy, to be merely watched by the faithful, but that these also should be drawn into the action. They are not to be "silent and detached spectators" but actual participants.

The Holy Father has expressly provided for the point here, and in a very striking manner, by ordering that this part of the service is to be done in the people's own tongue. The vernacular has thus been officially introduced into the liturgy. It enables us, as a community of brethren, to testify to each other that we explicitly and corporately undertake to fulfil those obligations which are inherent in our Baptism. We proclaim our realization of the fact that we all belong in one Body, which is the Body of Christ, His Church upon earth.

The priest invites us to renew our vows by addressing to us a short speech made up of words taken partly from St. Paul and partly from a sermon by St. Augustine.

Holding the candles which should remind us of the "burning light" given to us at our original Baptism, we then renew the vows made on our behalf by our Godparents. And afterwards we recite together the "Our Father," that prayer which may only be said by the baptized, and which was, in the early days of the Church, kept secret from those who were not members. It was taught to the catechumens just before their Baptism, and recited by them for the first time at the moment when they were made brethren of Christ and of each other. The "Our Father" is a baptismal prayer.

The central idea of the whole Vigil—comprising the festival of light, the prophecies and the baptismal ceremonies—is that this is the fulfilment in us of the original Jewish passover, of which it reproduces all the salient features.

But it still awaits a fulfilment of its own at the Parousia. Its purpose, therefore, is to constitute the true chosen people, faithful to the new alliance here below where, delivered from the slavery of Satan, this people shall await the day when they may pass over with the victorious Christ into the Kingdom of His Father, the true promised land.

Now let us look at the ceremonies for the blessing of the font.

(Read through the text which begins on p. 148, and make any comments which suggest themselves. Most of them are obvious, but a few are given here by way of samples.)

"May the Spirit impregnate this water." Cf. descent of the Spirit at Christ's own baptism. Words of our Lord to Nicodemus. Spirit over the waters at the first creation. This is the "new creation."

"Stainless womb." The Church is our mother; she is continually fruitful in new life she brings forth from the font.

"With blood from His side." The Fathers see in this the birth of the Church, Bride of Christ the Second Adam, as

He slept the sleep of death, resembling the birth of Eve, bride of the first Adam, as he was sleeping.

"Bless this water with Thy breath." Holy Ghost, Creator Spirit. God breathed life into Adam. The way through the Red Sea was cleared by "a strong and burning wind" (Ex. 24:21). At Pentecost the Holy Spirit came "as a strong wind blowing."

Paschal Candle lowered into the font. Christ descended into the Jordan.

"new childhood." Cf. "joy to my youth" at beginning of Mass. We participate in the Mass only in virtue of our Baptism. Priesthood of the laity.

Chapter Eight

OF THE PASCHAL MASS

The paschal Vigil concludes with the Mass of the Resurrection. In view of the contents and the purpose of the Vigil, no other conclusion is reasonably possible. For the baptized have been aggregated into the Mystical Body of Christ of which the primary function here below is to offer the Mass—to show forth the death of the Lord "until He comes."

Wherefore, the baptized, marked with the character which, in the words of St. Thomas Aquinas, is "a deputation to worship," and thus endowed with a participation in the priesthood of Christ the High Priest, should forthwith exercise that priesthood by taking their due part in sacrifice. And all who have been waiting for the coming of the Lord will desire that He may come now sacramentally if He is not going to appear visibly.

In every Mass when we "eat this Bread and drink this Cup we show forth the death of the Lord until He comes." But that thought should be especially vivid in our minds during the paschal Mass. For our Lord, at the Last Supper, said to His apostles: "With desire I have desired to eat this Pasch with you before I suffer. For I say to you that from this time I will not eat it until it be fulfilled in the kingdom of God" (Luke 22:15).

He is now celebrating His eternal Pasch in the kingdom of glory; we are not yet with Him above, but we should long to share it with Him when He comes again. Meanwhile we can eat of it sacramentally; we eat of the true Paschal Lamb who is in heaven, even though we ourselves are on earth.

That is the wonderful thing which the Eucharist does for us—it bridges the gap between time and eternity. For already we are living the life which is eternal life; we are living it now in time, but it will continue in eternity. Our Lord said, "He that eats my flesh and drinks my blood has everlasting life, and I will raise him up in the last day."

He did not say: "He who eats My flesh *will* have eternal life"; He said "he *has* eternal life." So we, who eat of the flesh of the Paschal Lamb have it already; we are even now living the life which is eternal.

Indeed we are living it at present in the world of time; but when time comes to an end, when He raises us up on the last day, then we shall live that life in eternity. But it is essentially the same life which we now have.

No wonder that at this Mass we shout out with joy the triumphant cry *Alleluia*. St. Jerome once wrote: "A new Man came into the world; a new law was given, a new people called into being through Baptism. Sing to Him a new song, for He is risen and He sits at the right hand of the Father!"

The *Alleluia* is the Church's Easter song of victory, sung here below, but in union with the never-ending *Alleluia* of those who celebrate the eternal Pasch of the Lamb in heaven above.

The door of heaven is opened; and though we may not enter through it until Christ appears again and invites us, "Come ye blessed of My Father," we can nevertheless hear with the ears of our soul the exultant song of those above. For at our Baptism the priest touched our ears and said to us, "*Ephpheta*—be thou opened."

We, the baptized, have been given spiritual hearing; and there comes to us through the open door of heaven the strains of that great multitude which St. John heard in his apocalyptic vision singing: "*Alleluia.* Salvation and power and glory belong to our God; *Amen, alleluia.* And there was a noise as of a great multitude, like the noise of water in flood, as they cried out: *Alleluia,* the Lord our God, the Almighty has claimed His kingdom. Let us rejoice and triumph and give Him praise; the time has come for the wedding feast of the Lamb. *Alleluia.*"

The Paschal Lamb stands at the center of the heavenly liturgy, as He does of our earthly liturgy. What St. John saw in heaven is but the fulfilment of what we do here on earth. As the deacon sang in his *Exsultet:* "This is the night wherein heaven is wedded to earth, and God to man." By our paschal Mass we are truly joining in, though sacramentally, with the Nuptials of the Lamb above.

In the Mass of this Easter night is enfolded, in mysterious fashion, everything which preceded it; all the meaningful rites and prayers about the paschal candle, the prophecies, the font, the sacrament of Baptism and the renewal of baptismal vows reach in this Mass their fitting conclusion.

By our participation in it we are caught up into the glory of the Risen Christ; in Him it shines forth; in us, not yet—but it is there. "You have died," says St. Paul to us in the Epistle, "and your life is hidden with Christ in God. When Christ, your life, shall appear, then you too will appear with Him in glory."

Another heartening message comes to us in the Gospel of the Mass. "Late in the night of the Sabbath, as the first day of the week began to dawn, Mary Magdalen and the other Mary came to see the sepulchre." We are there with them in spirit, "late on the night of the Sabbath, as the first day of the week" is beginning and drawing towards dawn. We too receive the message of the angels: "Do not be afraid; for I know that you seek Jesus who was crucified. He is not here, for He has risen even as He said."

Yes, we too seek Jesus who was crucified and who has risen; we seek Him—and we find Him in our paschal Communion. And being joined to Him and to each other we can find adequate expression of our happiness in singing together the Church's morning praise of Lauds, with its *Alleluia* antiphons and its psalm, "Praise the Lord all you nations."

And how fittingly there is chanted in the early hours of Easter Day that song which stood at the very beginning of our redemption—the *Benedictus*. At this time and on this occasion the richness of its content and its beauty must strike us with unwonted forcefulness. "Blessed be the Lord, the God of Israel, because He has visited and wrought redemption for His people . . . as He promised through the mouth of His prophets of old. . . ."

Yes, the Orient, the One who rose in the East, Christ the Sun of Justice has indeed visited us; He has shone on those who sat in darkness; He has guided our feet in the way of peace.

And so we pray in the Postcommunion: "Pour out the Spirit of Thy love into our hearts, O Lord, that those whom Thou hast nourished with the Easter sacraments may, because of Thy love, dwell together in peace." And we ask this in the Name of our Lord Jesus Christ, that Name before which "all who are in heaven and on earth and under the earth must bend the knee; for every tongue must confess that Jesus Christ is the Lord, dwelling in the glory of God the Father" (Phil. 3:8).

(Now page through the text of the Mass, making any comments that seem called for. A few suggestions follow.)

"Glory to God in the highest." At one time the *Gloria* was sung only at the Easter Mass which terminates the Vigil.

Later it was extended to Sunday Masses, because Sunday is a "little Easter." Only allowed at Bishop's Masses. Later still extended to Christmas and to other feasts, and allowed in Masses celebrated by priests. But this occasion—in the Vigil Mass—represents the earliest usage of the *Gloria* within the Mass.

Collect. Read it from page 164 and note its baptismal content, regarded primarily under its social aspect—"new children of Thy family." The two themes of resurrection and baptism are combined.

Offertory. Reflect especially on the *"Deus qui humanae substantiae"* with reference to Baptism.

Preface. Read the whole of it (page 169). Comment on phrase: "Who by dying has destroyed our death, and by rising has repaired our loss of life."

Hanc igitur. Point out the unwonted change in its content, referring to Baptism, page 171.

Unde et memores, page 171. Notice the phrase *"blessed* passion" and emphasize that every Mass commemorates the entire passover—resurrection and ascension as well as passion and death.

(For singing practice go over everything on pp. 56, 57, 58 and 59; and after that do a brief repetition of anything else the people may have to sing during Holy Week and which seems in special need of practice. Probably the Palm Sunday chants, and the *Venite adoremus* of Good Friday will require attention.)

APPENDIX ONE

Travelling around as much as I do, and meeting so many priests, I am in a position to pick up many ideas; also I read a great deal about what is actually done in America, England, France, Belgium, Holland, Germany and Austria. Hence the practical suggestions I am about to make are not mere idealistic theories; nor are they inventions of my own (though I have had opportunity of trying out almost everything I shall mention).

I set them forth here in the hope that priests who have to organize Holy Week services will find them useful and will personally try them. Clearly not all these suggestions can be adopted in every church, but each priest is likely to find something he could use to supplement his own methods.

Some general considerations

In the periodicals of several countries there have been published many articles dealing with the restored Holy Week services, some of them being reports of the conclusions reached at meetings of priests who have come together for the purpose of discussing practical aspects. In addition there are several books, of which two deserve special mention as being extremely helpful: *An Analysis of the Restored Holy Week Rites,* from the University of Notre Dame, Indiana, U.S.A., and *La Semaine Sainte* by Dom Thierry Maertens O.S.B. from the Abbey of St. Andre, Bruges, Belgium.

From all these sources one gathers that there is general agreement on the principle that where any service is clearly divisible into parts, then it is lawful to have one part sung while another part is merely said. For example, the Procession on Palm Sunday can be done with singing, and yet followed by a Low Mass without singing; or the Good Friday Liturgy may be said until the end of the Passion, and be a sung service from the Bidding Prayers onwards. Also, whenever anything is chanted by the deacon, subdeacon or lector, its text should not be read "privately" by the celebrant; this is explicitly stated in the rubrics as regards the Mass. And outside the Mass itself (such as at the Palm Sunday procession and the Paschal Vigil) the celebrant should not read anything except what he is explicitly told to read. Thus he would not read the *Pueri Hebraeorum* and psalms of Palm Sunday, nor the responsories after the lessons of Good Friday, nor the *Improperia* nor the canticles after the lessons of Holy Saturday, for all these are supplied by the choir.

Many commentators draw attention to the repeated insistence of the rubrics on the active participation of the people. Not only do the Decree and the Instruction make it clear that popular participation is one of the chief aims of the reform, but also the rubrics explicitly mention the same point again and again. Such phrases as *Cui omnes respondent, Respondent omnes, Omnes respondent* occur with significant frequency; there are many instances where even the simple word *Amen* at the end of a prayer has not been printed just with the usual symbol ℟ but is preceded by *Omnes* ℟ printed in red. Such directives did not appear in the liturgical texts drawn up in the days when popuar external participation in the sacred rites was unknown. But commentators point out that for some fifty years the Holy See has been urging and exhorting the clergy to let the people give the responses and sing the chants which rightly belong to them, and deduce that this has become an obligation during Holy Week since the principle of active participation has now been officially and authoritatively incorporated into the rubrics of this latest liturgical book.

Another point which emerges is the importance attached to the period for private prayer now prescribed after the *Flectamus genua* of the solemn collects on Good Friday and Holy Saturday. All are agreed that the command *Levate* must not be given until the purpose of the rubric can have been fulfilled, that is, until it shall have been reasonably possible for the faithful to have devoted themselves to private prayer. And most of the commentators seem to think that this could not be done in a period of time less than that needed for the recitation of the *Pater noster*. They say also that celebrant and people should kneel on both knees during this pause.

There has also been discussion as to whether vernacular hymns may be sung during the Palm Sunday procession after the *Gloria laus et honor*. The severest opinion I have been able to find in any of these books and articles is "No, unless the bishop expressly allows it"; the most liberal opinion is a simple, unqualified "Yes"; the usual opinion is "Yes, unless the bishop has expressly forbidden it." In any case it is an incontestible fact that vernacular hymns in honour of Christ the King were sung in the Palm Sunday processions of 1956 in very many (probably the majority) of parishes throughout Germany and France, as appears from reports in the liturgical journals. I have personal knowledge of not a few parishes in the United States and in England where this was done; and one of our own bishops, pontificating in his own cathedral, told the choir to start up "Hail Redeemer, King Divine." I know this because he told me so himself.

Palm Sunday.

The Ordinances of February 1, 1957, allow one to have the Blessing and Distribution of Palms in some place other than the church, and then to go in procession to the church for Mass. No one who has yet to try this plan can have any conception of how effective it is; it richly repays the bit of trouble involved in setting up a temporary altar elsewhere and causing the people to assemble in that place.

Most parishes have their school near enough to the church to render it possible. The first part of the service could be held in the Assembly Hall or the largest of the schoolrooms or even in the Entrance Foyer. If the arrangements are announced on the Fourth Sunday of Lent and again on Passion Sunday, the people will take due notice because of their novelty. Nevertheless it is a good plan to post a couple of men at the door of the church, that they may re-direct to the place of assembly any who go to the church in error.

According to the new rubrics it is now lawful for the people to bring with them their own branches (which need not be palms, but could be yew or laurel or willow from local sources); or they may be given branches (palms or otherwise) as they go in. They can hold the branches in their hands during the blessing. In that case there would be no distribution to the people during the singing of the *Pueri Hebraeorum,* but only to the sacred ministers and servers (and perhaps the choir?) whose branches must be placed on the *abacum, tobalea alba coopertum* of rubric 4. For a large congregation such a procedure would save much time. But where the congregation is not enormous it would seem better to bless their branches on the table and have a distribution. For this would give an opportunity to the people to sing, at least a few times, the chorus of the *Pueri Hebraeorum,* and thus be stimulated into the right mood for the procession. It is surely desirable to get the people to sing whenever possible, and as this chant is quite easy it seems a pity to have a distribution so short that the singing is practically eliminated. Even with larger congregations it is possible to have a distribution of moderate length.

The procession should be as grand and significant as possible, with all the people walking in it, as a tribute to Christ the King. It ought to go out of doors, by some fairly long way—as will be the case if it can start from the parish hall or school. But even if it has to start from the church and come back to the church, it should go outside and everybody should be in it, carrying branches and singing as well as they know how. If they proceed in a long thin line, two abreast, the singing is likely to be poor. Far better if there be ushers to marshal them four abreast as soon as they are outside; and obviously they should know what they are expected to sing, and should have copies at least of the words.

But what can be done if the church is packed with people who cannot be led outside either because it is pouring with rain or because the church door opens into a busy city street filled with traffic? Then there is nothing for it to have a procession around the aisles; and manifestly not all the people can circulate in this! However, even in such a token procession, there should surely be included a dozen or a score of the laity, such as representatives of the various parish confraternities. And all the people, though confined to their benches, should join in the singing.

An important point concerns the termination of this part of the service. The celebrant, from the predella, and facing the people, is to greet them all with a *Dominus vobiscum* and sing a concluding prayer. It would be most unseemly if he were to do this prematurely, while people were still entering the benches. Because he is at the head of the procession he will reach his place long before others reach theirs, and hence will have to exercise Christian virtue of patience until all the people are in their pews.

As regards preaching during the Holy Week services, the only sermon explicitly recommended in the rubrics is that which should follow the Gospel on Holy Thursday. But commentators are agreed that it is permitted to preach also at other suitable times, and suggest that before the Palm Sunday procession and before the Veneration of the Cross on Good Friday are such occasions. For priests who think likewise, some material for the purpose is given here in Appendix III.

For the Mass the new rubrics make it clear that it is lawful to read (rather than sing) the Passion even when it is, in other respects, a Sung Mass. No doubt the singing of the Passion invests the whole with a great dignity and is impressive in its way. The people, however, are then left with no help except their books (if they have any) from which they will have to read the Passion for themselves.

But if the Passion is going to be said, there is opportunity for the public reading of its translation while the celebrant reads the Latin quietly at the altar. This can, of course, be done by a single reader, but it is far more effective if it be done by a team of three, who speak the parts of *Chronista, Christus,* and *Synagoga* as apportioned to the three deacons when the Passion is sung.

Maundy Thursday

We used to have great crowds of children at the morning Mass, but very few adults. Now, thanks to the reform, we have crowds of adults at the evening Mass, but very few children. It is too late for them, and in most churches there would not be room for them as well as for the adults. What can we do for the children?

In the *Instructio,* n.17, it is explicitly laid down that the Ordinary may permit a Low Mass, in addition to the official *Missa Solemna Verspertina in Cena Domini,* wherever there is a *ratio pastoralis*. Might not the solution lie in asking permission from the bishop to have, at 5 p.m., a Low Mass to which there would be admitted only the children and such adults as may have to be there to take charge of them? They would all have finished their dinners well before 2 p.m.; they could still have liquid sustenance until 4 p.m., and would get their evening meal at 6 p.m. or soon afterwards.

Presumably the rubrics and the Proper of this Mass would be exactly the same as those for the later public Mass (seeing that the new *Ordo* has replaced the *Missale Romanum* during the whole week). There would, of course, be no Mandatum; and n.17 of the rubrics provides for the conclusion of this extra Mass *more solito*, i.e. with *Ite*, blessing and Last Gospel. But there is no indication that rubric n.1. does not apply; which means that the tabernacle must be empty to begin with, and that the children must be given hosts consecrated at that same Mass. Hence it is important to know the number required as exactly as possible so that none may be left over at the end of Mass.

The most certain way to ensure this is to have, at the back of the church, a table bearing an open ciborium and a box of hosts. Before Mass each child, on entering, transfers a host from the box to the ciborium. The filled ciborium is then placed on the altar just before the Mass begins or, better still, is carried up at the Offertory (on a tray), received by a server at the altar gates, and taken up to the celebrant who places it on the corporal. This procedure breaks no rubrics whatever, for it makes no difference to the actions of the priest. And it fulfills not only the requirements but also the purpose indicated by the Pope in n.126 of *Mediator Dei* wherein the practice of "receiving particles consecrated at the same Mass" is commended, namely, "that it may be more evident that by receiving Holy Communion the faithful take part in the sacrifice."

The only other point to note is the *severitas* commended

in the *Instructio* II.9. concerning the decoration of the Altar of Repose. A few candles and flowers are in order, but not the elaborate horticultural display that was customary hitherto.

Good Friday

The question arises as to whether there ought to be continuous adoration before the Altar of Repose all the morning. The Instructio II.10 says that on the previous evening it is to be *protrahenda saltem usque ad mediam noctem*. These words, it seems to me, mean only what they say; there *must* be public adoration until midnight. There is no prohibition of adoration after that time; there would be nothing wrong in having it, but equally nothing wrong in omitting it. But if it is done, the spirit of it should change; it is no longer concerned with the institution of the Blessed Sacrament, but instead with "the memory of the passion and death of the Lord."

So if some priest decided to have a sort of "Holy Hour" at the Altar of Repose during Good Friday morning he would be acting correctly provided it were not the usual sort of "Eucharistic" Holy Hour but, instead, an Hour concerned in some way with the Passion. There would seem no objection to Stations of the Cross on Good Friday morning; they are certainly in the right spirit. And it was, after all, on Good Friday morning that our Lord was actually carrying His Cross.

For the Solemn Liturgy at noon (or later if circumstances warrant this), it is very helpful to have a commentary such as that suggested in Appendix II of this book. The Passion, when not sung, can be done by a single Lector or by a team of three as described above for Palm Sunday.

The rubrics say that the Cross used for the Veneration must be *satis magna*. After it has been unveiled it has to be held by two acolytes with its foot on the predella. That should give an indication of its minimum size; it ought not to be so small that they have to bend down to hold its arms, and the feet of the *Corpus* should be so high from the ground that the priest, when kneeling just below the top step, will be able to kiss them without inconvenience. In practice any Crucifix less than four feet high will be found inconvenient. It is much easier to kiss it if the acolytes hold it tilting backwards, not vertically.

All commentators are agreed that, for veneration by the people, additional Crucifixes may be used. The people are to come up in procession, making a single genuflexion before kneeling to kiss the Crucifix. The choir should sing the *Improperia,* but there is no need for the priest to read them himself. Because this veneration takes a long time the people are apt to be bored if they have nothing to do but sit and listen to the choir singing the reproaches over and over again. It is therefore quite important that they should be taught to sing the chorus of the *Crux fidelis* so that they can join in after each verse by the choir. Personally I see no reason why they should not also sing *Vexilla Regis* which has now been eliminated from the procession which brings the Blessed Sacrament back from the Altar of Repose. The 1957 Ordinances permit the adoration of the Cross by the people *en masse,* instead of individually, when the crowds are so great that good order and devotion would be endangered.

Another point of the highest importance is to get the people to join in the *Pater noster* of the Communion service. The rubric is very specific: "all present, both clergy and faithful, are to recite the *Pater noster* together with the celebrant solemnly, with dignity and distinctly, in the Latin tongue." They will do it well enough if they are properly led, especially if they have books mentioned on pages 13-14.

While we must rejoice at the fact that the people may receive Holy Communion on Good Friday, there is no denying that it has its difficulties. The 1957 Ordinance noted above is definitely helpful. The coming and going may have lasted half an hour or more. And hardly have the people got back into their benches when they are stirred up yet again to come to the altar rails for Communion. This may well take another twenty minutes to half an hour in a big church. So that, out of the whole time which the service takes, anything up to an hour may be occupied in coming and going. It seems a pity that those who devised this part of the rite did not model it on the practice in vogue in ninth-century Gaul. The veneration of the Cross was then combined with Communion; each person kissed the Cross and was immediately given its sacred Victim before returning to his place. Thus there was only one procession. As things are we must endeavor to make this second procession seem less long by any means we can devise. The choir is supposed to sing Ps. 21 during the distribution, but it is most unlikely that the people will ever learn to join in a long Latin psalm which occurs but once a year. It might help them if a translation of each pair of verses were read out by the Lector before the choir sings the corresponding Latin.

The Paschal Vigil

The most practical plan for the beginning seems to be that the people should assemble in the lighted church, each collecting a candle and a book on the way in. Again I would recommend the booklet published by the Liturgical Press, Collegeville. A couple of altar boys could be on duty to issue books and candles to all who enter; a third could brandish a money-box or collecting basket labelled "Offerings for Candles" if the parish finances are such that they need that assistance.

Unless bad weather or considerations of space render it impossible, the people should witness the Blessing of New Fire and of the Paschal Candle outside the church. Accordingly, when it is time to start, the Commentator should tell them all to go outside and stand in a ring round the New Fire which, having been lit a short while before, ought by then to be burning merrily.

Let it be a real big fire, burning brightly with plenty of flames, not just a miserable glow of a few bits of charcoal in the bottom of some old disused thurible. A large brazier, like those things that night watchmen sit over when extensive street repairs are in progress, makes a splendid receptacle. If it is filled with some paper, then shavings mixed with those bits of wax that have been scraped off guttering candles, then pieces of a broken wooden packing case, and finally a few bits of dry timber, it will blaze up into a fire that really deserves the solemn blessing of the Church. It does not have to be lit in the presence of the people, but can be set going five or ten minutes before the service begins.

From this fire the charcoal for the censer is to be lighted. It can be easily done by means of a small wire basket three or four inches in diameter on the end of a long wire handle. Any handy-man could make such an object in a few minutes out of a length of stiff fence-wire and a bit of wire netting. The charcoal is put into the basket which itself rests on top of the fire to be lit, with its handle projecting outside. When the right moment comes, a server simply takes hold of the handle, lifts out the basket, and tips its glowing contents into the thurible.

The priest and his attendants come last of all out of the church which is now empty except for somebody who will have been detailed to turn out all the lights. The Commentator should remember to have with him an electric torch by means of which he can read the bit of "copy" that is his business while outside the church.

The people come back in procession following the Paschal

Candle; the third *Lumen Christi* is not sung until the people are all back in their pews. It is surprising how quickly they get back; they take far less time than one would expect. The third candle-lighting is also quite a short affair if it be arranged that a team of a dozen altar boys, who will have lit their candles at the second *Lumen Christi,* disperse at the third salutation to predetermined points in the church, and from those points spread their lights among the people.

The Vigil ceremony makes explicit provision for the administration of Baptism, and where this can be done it greatly adds to the effectiveness of the whole rite. It happens not infrequently that there is, under instruction, some convert whose reception into the Church could be arranged for the occasion. It is lawful to do all the preliminaries beforehand, for instance, in the morning *(Instructio II. 14);* and the Baptism is administered, not in the Baptistery (to which the newly blessed water has not yet been carried) but in the sanctuary, where all can see.

The question put to, and the answers received from, the candidate should be loud and clear so that everyone may hear them. At the injunction "Receive this white robe" the candidate might put on an alb (if a man) or a white cloak (if a woman); and after receiving the candle lighted from the Paschal candle and told to "Go in peace" the neophyte should be led to a place of honour in the front bench.

At the renewal of baptismal vows by all the congregation, everyone will be holding a lighted candle. These candles will be held at elbow-height (the natural position) during the preliminary address. If the people are told beforehand to lift up their candles high when they make the first answer "We do", and to keep them held up until invited to recite the Our Father, the effect is most striking; the whole appearance of the church seems to be transformed by a blaze of light when the candles are raised. It is even more effective if all the electric lights are put out when the people have lit their candles before the address "Dearly beloved brethren", and not turned on again until the final "Amen" of the renewal ceremony.

Another good hint concerns the end of the Vigil. It seems incongruous for the Prophecies and Blessing of the baptismal Water to take place against a background of an altar festively decorated with a white frontal and adorned with flowers. Yet to rush all these things onto the altar at the last possible moment, during the second part of the Litanies, is highly inconvenient.

The problem can be solved in some churches where the walls or pillars round the sanctuary permit of it, by the following plan: rig up a strong wire, fairly high up, from one wall of the sanctuary to the other, approximately over the spot where the priest stands for the *Judica* of a Mass. Suspend from this wire a lightweight purple curtain, to hide the entire altar from view. Then the altar, in all its glory, can be prepared at leisure during the day. The curtains make an admirable background for the *Exsultet* and all the rest of the Vigil service. Then, as the *Kyrie* is intoned at the end of the Litany, two altar boys pull strings which cause the curtains to part in the middle and be drawn to the ends of the wire, exposing the altar to view.

The "transformation scene" from the sombre purple background of the Vigil to the festive altar resplendent with lights and flowers is so effective that it draws gasps of delight from the populace. Undoubtedly this bit of "drama" is in the spirit of the occasion. I have done it in two different churches, and each time it was the subject of pleased comments afterwards.

Another point concerns the bell-ringing for the *Gloria*. We should not be content with a mere token tinkling of a single *campanella;* let all available bells be collected from side altars, presbytery dinner tables or other possible sources, and issued to numerous altar boys with instructions to shake the very tongues out of them when the priest intones *Gloria;* let the organist pull out his tubas and mixtures and superoctave couplers and thirty-two foot reeds and really prance about for all he is worth. *Laudate Dominum in sanctuario ejus . . . laudate eum cum clangore tubae . . . laudate eum chordis et organo . . . laudate eum cymbalis crepitantibus* (Ps. 150); that is the spirit; plenty of *clangor* and *crepitatio* for fifteen joyous seconds! The altar boys love it—so do the people.

MATERIAL PREPARATIONS.

This book is not a sacristan's manual, nor a guide to masters of ceremonies. Doubtless books of that type will be published soon, if indeed they are not already available. But it may be useful here to give some brief indications of the things which have to be got ready for the Holy Week Services according to the Restored Rites. I do not claim that they are absolutely complete.

Palm Sunday

Remember that the liturgical colour for the blessing of the branches is now red. The celebrant will need a red cope, and the other ministers will need a red dalmatic and tunicle. If no red cope is available the ceremony may be done according to the simple rite by the celebrant dressed in alb and red stole.

A table covered with a white cloth will be needed to hold the branches that are to be blessed for the sacred ministers and altar staff (at least); it must be placed centrally, where it can be seen by the people, as the celebrant is to function from behind it, facing the people. He will need the Holy Water bucket and aspersory, also thurible and incense, and a basin of water with soap and towel to wash his hands after the distribution. The processional Cross is to *un*veiled. Purple vestments have to be prepared for the Mass.

Maundy Thursday

Before Mass the tabernacle is to be empty, and white vestments should be got ready. Only one large host to be put on the paten. The additional chalice with white veil and tapes formerly in use is now abolished, since it is the ciborium which will henceforth be carried to the Altar of Repose after the Mass.

The ciborium must contain as many altar-breads as are judged necessary for the people's Communion of both Maundy Thursday and Good Friday. It may well be that more than one ciborium will be required.

Commentators differ about the colour of the veil for the altar-Crucifix. There is no mention of it in the new rubrics. Some argue that this indicates no change from the former practice, when the veil was white. Others argue that it means no change from the purple veil in use from Passion Sunday onwards.

Surplices and white stoles to be available for any priests who may be assisting in choir. Purple stoles to be ready for celebrant and deacon when they are stripping the altar afterwards.

A white cope and humeral veil should be ready for the procession; also candles for torch-bearers, canopy, processional Cross (veiled), thurible.

Good Friday

The altar is completely denuded—no Cross, no candles, no altar cloths and (if possible) no carpets in the sanctuary. The tabernacle empty and open.

Until the end of the Passion the sacred ministers wear amice, alb and girdle; celebrant and deacon wear black stoles, but the subdeacon does not. For the Bidding prayers the celebrant puts on a black cope, while the deacon and subdeacon put on black dalmatic and tunicle respectively. These should be available near the Sedilia. The rubrics make no mention of maniples. Cope, dalmatic and tunicle are removed for the Adoration of the Cross. After it, for the Communion service, the sacred ministers put on (rather incongruously) purple Mass vestments, but without maniples. One wonders why the celebrant is not directed to wear a purple cope, since this is not a Mass. Purple stoles will be needed for the priests in choir.

The big Crucifix should be prepared, veiled, in the sacristy; also candles for the acolytes. On a credence table should be an altar cloth, a burse containing a corporal, a vessel of water and finger cloth to be put on the altar for the priest to purify his fingers after distributing Communion. At the Altar of Repose should be a white humeral veil, the *umbella,* and a pair of acolytes' candles (additional to those used during the Adoration of the Cross).

Holy Saturday

Near the fire (or in the church porch ready to be carried to the fire) a table should be prepared with a white cloth. On it lay out a white dalmatic, stole and maniple; the Paschal Candle with suitable sharp instrument; a dish with the incense grains; incense boat; a taper; an *Ordo Hebdomadae Sanctae Instauratus;* and sufficient small candles for the celebrant and altar staff.

In the porch or narthex of the church should be a supply of candles and books to be issued to the incoming faithful. Money box if offerings for candles are going to be taken up.

The altar to be prepared for Mass. If a purple curtain is to be used, all decorations can be done beforehand. If not, all things needed must be hidden in some nearby place, and arrangements made to rush them on at the last moment.

The Credence table should bear a chalice prepared for Mass, with white veil and burse, all covered with a white humeral

APPENDIX TWO

There can be little doubt that the people, even if they have texts in their hands, are much helped by a few words of commentary (they should be few!) inserted into the Holy Week services here and there. There is an evocative power in the spoken word which works to bring the service to life, to rally the powers of attention, and to remove that sense of "being lost" which so often afflicts a congregation present at a function that is not utterly familiar.

But if a priest attempts to comment without carefully preparing beforehand just when he will speak and precisely what he is going to say, there is danger of unduly frequent interruption of the ceremony, prolixity and poverty of content. In order to help priests make their own commentaries, I venture to offer as samples those which I have used myself on Palm Sunday, Maundy Thursday, Good Friday and Holy Saturday.

For those people who came to the preparatory instructions these comments serve to remind them of what they have heard. For the rest a minimum of instruction and guidance is provided, to make the functions intelligible.

If any priest desires to use the commentaries as they stand here, he is, of course, very welcome to do so. And others who have to conduct Holy Week Services all by themselves may find it useful to have these commentaries read out, at the appropriate moments, by some reliable layman.

PALM SUNDAY

Before the beginning.

This morning we are going to re-enact the triumphal procession which accompanied Our Lord as He entered Jerusalem a few days before He suffered for us. The Jews waved palm-branches and shouted *Hosannas* in His honour; and so we too will carry branches and sing the praises of Our Saviour as we walk along. The priest begins the ceremonies by blessing the branches we are to carry.

Before the distribution.

While the priest gives out the blessed branches we sing the antiphon about the Jewish children who carried olive-branches and shouted *Hosanna.* Join in this antiphon after each verse sung by the choir.

When the distribution is finished.

We shall now hear the Gospel account of the occasion we are calling to mind.

(If the Gospel is sung, read its translation immediately afterwards. If the Gospel is only said, read the translation concurrently).

At the end of the Gospel (if there is no sermon).

Having heard that story of long ago, we make it come true again now. Carrying our branches, and singing in honour of Christ our King, we take part in the procession that will enter our Church which represents Jerusalem.

After the procession, just before its concluding prayer.

In the prayer which follows we ask of Christ Our King, in whose honour we have carried these branches and sung our hymns, that these branches may bring His blessing upon our homes in which we shall place them.

(No commentary during the Mass).

MAUNDY THURSDAY

Before the beginning of the Mass.

What we are about to do is officially entitled "The Mass of the Lord's Supper." We remember the great love which our Lord showed on the night before He suffered, by washing the feet of His disciples, giving the commandment of mutual love, and instituting the Holy Eucharist, sacrament of love. The altar is adorned with flowers as a sign of joy in this great gift. The tabernacle is empty; the hosts we shall receive in Communion will be consecrated at this Mass in order that we may share as closely as possible in this sacrifice of Christian unity.

After the sermon, if the Maundy ceremony is to be done.

What Our Lord did just before He instituted the Mass will be done again now by the priest before he celebrates the Mass of the Last Supper. It should help us to realize that true Christian charity should make us always ready to serve one another, even in humble ways, and that the priesthood is a sacred office involving service to God's people.

Just before the Agnus Dei.

Judas betrayed our Lord with a kiss. To remind us of that fact, the Kiss of Peace is omitted at this Mass. Hence the third *Agnus Dei* is not followed by *dona nobis pacem* as is usual, but—like the other two—by *miserere nobis.*

After the Agnus Dei

Usually the Communions of the priest and of the people

are separated by the *Confiteor* and other prayers. Today, as a further sign of perfect union in Christ, these prayers are omitted. The priest gives to the people their share of the sacrifice immediately after his own, from the ciborium which he has just consecrated.

During the Placeat

Today we are not dismissed with the *Ite missa est* and blessing, for we remain now for the procession in which the Ciborium, needed for tomorrow's Communion, is carried to the Altar of Repose. All should join in the singing as best they can; and afterwards, from now until at least midnight, there should be many who come to adore Our Lord in the Sacrament of His love. It is the night of His agony, when He asked: "Could you not watch one hour with Me?"

GOOD FRIDAY

Before the beginning.

Good Friday—the day of the Crucifixion! The Church is in mourning, for it is the anniversary of the death of her Spouse. The Cross on the altar is veiled in black; the priest wears black vestments. Yet we must not think of this as any kind of a funeral service; the powerful note of hope sounds through it all—hope in the Resurrection and in Eternal Life won through the Cross of Christ.

Before the first reading.

The reading from the Scriptures is taken from the Prophet Osee. He teaches us that God will judge severely those who turn to Him only in time of trouble, and fall away from His service when their troubles have passed.

Before the second reading.

Now comes a passage from the Book of Exodus, describing

the first liberation of Israel from the slavery of Egypt. The Paschal Lamb foreshadows Christ, the true Paschal Lamb. The blood of that lamb set the Jews free from slavery; the Blood of Christ sets us free from sin.

(There seems no need of any comment before the reading of the Passion.)

Before the Bidding Prayers.

Christ died for all men; we now pray for all men, through our great High Priest who, as St. Paul tells us, "by His own Blood entered once and for all into the sanctuary of His Father . . . there He now appears in God's sight on our behalf" (Hebr. 2). During the pauses, while we kneel down, we should all pray privately for the intention announced by the priest. The first prayer is "for the Church of God, that she may have peace and unity throughout the world."

(After each *Amen* the next intention may be briefly announced as follows: For the Pope. For the clergy and people. For converts under instruction. For all in trouble. For the conversion of non-Catholics. For the Jews. For pagans.)

After the last of these prayers.

Now we come to the Adoration of the Cross, the instrument of our salvation. We thus express our faith in the divinity of Christ who died on that Cross, and our gratitude to Him for having suffered so much. But the Cross is also the instrument of His triumph. By it He conquered Satan, He conquered sin, He conquered death. By His Cross He has given us the life of grace conferred in Baptism; it is the beginning of that eternal life which will be ours after the resurrection.

After the Venite Adoremus.

(If there are any directions to be given about coming to and going from the Kissing of the Cross, give them briefly here.) Then add: While waiting, before and after you have kissed the Cross, occupy your time reading and reflecting on the Reproaches, which the choir will sing.

After the Crux Fidelis.

We shall now have the privilege of receiving in Holy Communion the very Victim of the Cross; for this purpose the Ciborium is brought back from the Altar of Repose while the choir sings "We adore Thee, O Christ and we bless Thee, because by Thy Holy Cross Thou hast redeemed the world."

As soon as the choir has finished the antiphon.

We are to be united sacramentally with Christ who died for us. It is through His death that we have been made His brethren, adopted sons of the same Father. And so, to prepare for our Communion, we are permitted to say, as one united family of God, the *Pater noster,* in which the priest will lead us.

At the end of the whole ceremony.

During our Lord's life the disciples of John the Baptist came to Him and asked why His disciples did not fast. And He replied: "Can you expect the men of the bridegroom's company to go mourning when the bridegroom is still with them? No—but the day will come when the bridegroom is taken away from them; and then they will mourn and fast." That day has come for us; we mourn because the Bridegroom is taken away from His Spouse, the Church. The Tabernacle is empty; there is left to us only His Cross. So let us spend this day in a spirit of reverent sorrow, and of sympathy with our Mother the Church in her mourning. The more sincerely we do this today and tomorrow, the more joyously we shall be able to celebrate, tomorrow night, the great paschal Vigil, wherein our sorrow shall be turned into joy at His Resurrection.

THE PASCHAL VIGIL

At the very beginning.

The paschal Vigil is the climax of our celebration of the Christian Mysteries, for it is concerned with the Resurrection of Christ from His tomb, and also the resurrection of mankind, in Him and through Him, from the death of sin to the life of grace.

We start with the blessing of new fire, new light. Fire has been struck from a flint or rock; this reminds us how Christ, the Light of the world, came forth from the rock of His grave on this Holy Night, to enlighten those who "sat in the darkness and the shadow of death."

(As the people cannot read their books in the darkness, the reader should have with him a torch by the light of which he should read, after the priest's Latin, the prayer at the foot of page 128. All page references are to the booklet entitled *The Masses of Holy Week and the Easter Vigil,* published by The Liturgical Press, Collegeville, Minn. It is highly desirable that every person in the church should have a copy of this booklet.)

After the blessing of the fire.

The paschal Candle, the "great light" which signifies the Risen Christ, is brought to the priest who will bless it. He inscribes upon this candle a Cross; also the first and last letters of the Greek alphabet, which remind us that Christ is the beginning and end of all things. He also inscribes the figures indicating the current year, to remind us that this Year of Salvation, like all others, must be spent in the following of Christ.

(After each phrase spoken by the priest, the reader should interject its translation, since the people cannot read them and do not know Latin.)

While the priest blesses the Grains.

The priest blesses the five Grains of Incense which are to be fixed onto the Cross cut in the candle, to remind us of the five Wounds of Christ's passion and death, visible even in His glorified Body.

(Interject translation of phrases as before. If time permits, read translation of prayer, bottom of p. 129, after the priest's Latin.)

While the deacon puts on his dalmatic.

The deacon puts on his feast day vestments because he is going to be the first to announce to us officially the great joy of the Resurrection. We shall enter the darkened church in procession; and the lighted candle will go before us just as the Pillar of Fire went before the Israelites at their liberation from the slavery of Egypt.

After the Procession.

We all stand, holding our lighted candles, to hear the *Exsultet,* the great Easter Song. The deacon invites heaven and earth and the Church of God, and especially ourselves here present, to rejoice with him in the Resurrection of Christ and its consequences. While he sings you should read, with closest attention, the translation beginning on page 10 of your booklets.

After the Exsultet.

The Feast of Light is now finished. But with that light in our minds and hearts we are to begin the Vigil, or time of waiting. It is concerned with Baptism, through which the new life won for us by Christ has been given to our souls. In olden days this was the occasion on which new Christians were baptized, confirmed, and took part in their first Mass. Tonight we prepare ourselves to renew our baptismal vows by reflecting on certain readings from holy Scripture.

Before the first Prophecy.

God's creation of the world and of the human race described in the first prophecy were ruined by original sin. Through the disobedience of the First Adam the human race was delivered into the slavery of sin. But Christ is the Second Adam; through His obedience even to the death of the Cross we have been freed from that slavery. There has been a new creation, even more wonderful than the first creation recounted for us now.

Before the second Prophecy.

Now we shall hear how Israel was freed from the slavery of Egypt. The Jews were led through the waters of the Red Sea and became God's chosen people. We, too, are led through waters—those of Baptism; and thereby we become the new Chosen People destined for the true Promised Land of heaven. The deliverance of the Jews was called the Passover, or Pasch. That is why our deliverance—wrought for us by Christ—is called the Christian Pasch.

Before the third Prophecy.

The prophet Isaias speaks to us. He foretold the coming of Christ, and the holiness of the Church which He would found. The Church is made up of the baptized, who are purified and sanctified in the font.

Before the fourth Prophecy.

Now we hear the voice of Moses. Near the end of his life he exhorted the people ever to remain faithful to God's laws; for only thus would they find true happiness. That applies to us too; we shall promise to remain faithful to the laws which

Christ gave us when we renew our baptismal vows later this evening.

Before the first part of the Litanies.

We ask all the saints in heaven to unite with our paschal joy, and to pray for us that we may ever remain true to the grace of Baptism.

Before the Blessing of the Water.

During the coming year many will be given a share in the passion, death and resurrection of Christ by Baptism. The water which will be used for them is now to be blessed. As Christ descended into the grave and rose to newness of life, so now the paschal Candle, the symbol of Christ, will descend into the waters and rise up again. This reminds us that it is from Christ that these waters will have power to impart newness of life to those who will rise from the font, on their baptismal day, as new creatures freed from sin.

(At the appropriate moments the Lector might well read out the two short paragraphs on page 152: "May the power of the Holy Spirit . . ." and "And may He make the whole substance . . ."; also the first three short paragraphs on page 153: "May this font . . .," "May the inpouring of the Chrism . . .," "May this mingling of the Chrism . . .")

Before the second part of the Litanies.

In this second part of the Litanies we are reminded of the many reasons we have for confidence. Let us take special note of those invocations which run: "Through Thy Cross and Passion: through Thy Death and Burial: through Thy holy Resurrection."

At the end of the Litanies, but before the Kyrie, i.e., at top of p. 163.

Now we begin the Easter Mass—the Mass of Resurrection

and of Baptism. We rejoice in a historic fact of the *past*—that Christ rose from the dead. We rejoice in an actual fact of the *present*—that through Baptism we share His death and Resurrection. We look forward to a certain fact of the *future*—that Christ will come again to lead us into the eternal kingdom of His glory. That will be our final Passover, when all His redemptive work will be finished. In this Mass He anticipates His Second Coming, the Parousia, by coming to us in sacramental form, to give us a foretaste and a pledge of our own resurrection to eternal glory.

APPENDIX THREE

At the request of some of the clergy material is now provided for three sermons which can be preached, if desired, during the actual Holy Week Services. The first is intended for the Second Sunday in Passiontide or Palm Sunday just after the Gospel which follows the blessing of the branches, and before the actual procession. The second is intended for use on Holy Thursday after the Gospel of the Mass. The third is for Good Friday at the conclusion of the Bidding Prayers, before the Veneration of the Cross.

The Second Sunday in Passiontide or Palm Sunday

> *Those who followed kept crying out:* Hosanna! *Blessed is He that comes in the Name of the Lord!*—Matth. 21:8.

We know from carvings on the ancient monuments of Egypt and India that in those old civilizations great events were celebrated by processions. We know from classical history that when a Greek or Roman general had led his army to victory the triumph was celebrated by a procession. We know from the Old Testament that when the Ark of God was carried to Jerusalem King David and his people brought it there in a joyous procession. And if we look at the various countries and peoples of today we still find the same kind of thing: when they crown a monarch or open a parliament or celebrate an achievement they hold a procession. Does not all this show that a procession is something very natural, rooted in human nature and social instincts? It is not, in itself, anything specifically religious. But because it is so natural and instinctive it has found its way into the social celebration—that is, the liturgy—of every religion, including our own.

Very early in her history the Catholic Church made use of processions in her worship. We are just about to hold a procession which goes back at least as far as the fourth century; it is, in fact, based on the still earlier procession in which our Lord Himself was the central figure, as described in the Gospel passage just read to you.

And why do we hold this procession today? Because it is the first of the ceremonies of Holy Week, an entire week designated as "Holy" because it celebrates the most wonderful fact of human history. This is the fact that the Incarnate Son of God has redeemed sinful man and opened to him the gates of heaven. There is, indeed, infinite sadness in the story of how He did it, for He suffered and died for our sakes. On certain occasions during the week we shall steep ourselves in that sadness; in fact, we end on that note even today, with the Mass which includes the history of Christ's passion. But to begin with, the Church reminds us that all that is of the past. What is of the present, what is of the future, enduring to all eternity, is the joy of His achievement. He conquered sin and death, bringing to us grace and life. We are first of all to impress this on our minds in order that our hearts may glow with gratitude and our wills burn with desire to profit by what Christ has done for us. Even while we contemplate the sufferings and death of our Saviour we are never to lose sight of the end, of the glory which lies beyond.

In the decree which reformed the Holy Week Services the Pope told us that the liturgy of this week has a "special sacramental power and efficacy to foster the Christian life." This power will be at work in us in proportion to the fervour wherewith we take part in the rites. They have been changed somewhat in form, and their times have been altered from those which were customary, for the precise purpose of enabling the faithful to take part in them as actively as possible. You will be doing three things: you will be recalling the past, honouring Christ in the present, and anticipating the future.

You will be recalling the past. In the original procession of palms and olives the Hebrews acclaimed Christ our Lord as the Messiah. Not merely did He permit them to do this, but clearly He willed it, for He expressly sent two of His disciples ahead to find the ass' colt on which He desired to ride. He publicly accepted the title which was His by right—that of Messiah, Saviour—because He was about to begin the saving work of His passion, death and resurrection. "And those who followed kept crying out: Hosanna!" "Hosanna!" is a Hebrew word which means "Be now our Saviour; glory to him who is our Saviour!"

But you do more than recall the past. You will be honoring Christ in the present, for Christ is here now amongst us. He is present mystically in this gathering of members of His Mystical Body. He is present representatively in His priest who presides over us; He is present symbolically in the figure on the Cross which heads the procession. By your acclamations you manifest your loyalty to Christ your Saviour. You accompany Him to the Mass we are about to offer, that Mass which is concerned with His passion and death and sacramentally renews them. You acclaim Him who comes to suffer that He may bring us healing; you witness to Him who seems to fail that He may conquer; you salute Him who dies that He may bring us life. "Hosanna! Glory to our Saviour! Blessed is He who comes in the name of the Lord!"

And you will, as it were, be rehearsing for the future. For Christ the Saviour, Christ the victorious King, will one day come again. This procession of ours which recalls the day when Christ entered the earthly Jerusalem anticipates the day when He will lead us into the heavenly Jerusalem. We of the Church militant are even now marching towards that final meeting with our Saviour; we are even now engaged in collecting the palms of victories over ourselves and the olive branches of peace with our neighbor. All during this life we should be preparing to take our part in the triumphal procession which will bring to conclusion all the saving work of our victorious Messiah-King. The eternal gates will open; the King of Glory will enter. May He grant that all of us will then be with Him singing, as we sing today, *"Gloria laus et honor tibi sit!"* "All glory, praise and honor to Thee, Redeemer King." "Hosanna!" "Glory to our Saviour!" Amen.

HOLY THURSDAY

I have given them the privilege ... that while thou art in me, I may be in them, and so they may be perfectly made one.—John 17:22.

While every Mass should remind us of the Last Supper, this Mass which we are celebrating on Holy Thursday evening should do so with especial force. Let us go in spirit to the Cenacle, and imagine our Lord and Master reclining there with His Apostles about Him. He had invited them to eat with Him the ceremonial Paschal meal instituted by Moses so many years before to commemorate the events whereby the Chosen People had been freed from the slavery of Egypt.

Though the Gospels do not expressly say so, we can hardly doubt that our Lord celebrated the Pasch with His disciples in previous years. But this year there was a difference. He altered the usual ritual in some respects; He interrupted its early stages by rising from table to wash their feet; and two of its concluding features—the blessing and distribution of bread and wine—were given by Him a new reality, a new meaning and a new function which He willed to endure till the end of time.

The new reality was that the bread and wine became His

own Body and Blood which He would give for them on Calvary next day. The new meaning was that this rite should be the new Testament or Covenant between God and the new Chosen People; and the new function was to bring about the union with Himself and with one another of those whom He desired to constitute as the new Chosen People of God. The ancient rite of blessing and distributing bread and wine at the Pasch was to become the new rite of consecrating and distributing the Body and Blood of Christ in the Mass. "Do this," He said, "in memory of Me."

Why did our Lord institute the Mass and "hand it over" to His Church on the very night when He Himself was "handed over" by betrayal unto death? There are several reasons, each of which could be (and has been) the subject of innumerable sermons and books. But tonight we will concentrate our attention on one reason which is especially plain from the circumstances in which Christ gave us the Mass, as also from those in which the Church bids us celebrate it this evening, namely, that He wanted the Holy Eucharist to be a sacrament of fraternal unity. By the Eucharist we are to be made one with Him and one with each other.

Look, first, at the circumstances of institution. Our Lord chose for the occasion a fraternal meal with His Apostles, a meal which they alone were privileged to eat with Him because they were specially dear to Him. He told them clearly how much He loved them, how He had longed and longed to share this meal with them.

Then, passing from word to action, He demonstrated His love by performing for them a humble service: He, who was their Lord and Master, knelt down before each one of them and washed their feet.

After that, during supper, He gave them that loving discourse of which St. John has written down all that he could remember in four precious chapters of his Gospel. There is but little order in this last talk of our Lord; it gives no evidence of a carefully worked out train of thought such as appears in the Sermon on the Mount or the sermon wherein He promised the Bread from heaven. This talk is absolutely informal and spontaneous. "I have many things to say to you," He explained; and what He had to say was poured forth impulsively, with a sense of urgency, in the knowledge that this was His last chance to speak to them of the things nearest to His Heart. But, though He ranged over many subjects, there is one topic to which He kept recurring again and again under all sorts of different aspects—the subject of unity, of fraternal charity.

"I have a new commandment to give you," He said, "that you are to love one another; that your love for one another is to be like the love I have borne you." And again: "The mark by which all men will know you for my disciples will be the love you bear one another." He talked then of His going to the Father, and of the Holy Spirit, the Spirit of Love whom He would send; but soon was back on the old theme of love and union amongst themselves. "If any man has any love for me, he will be true to my word ... Peace is my bequest to you, and the peace which I give you is mine to give."

And then, as a sign of His own love for them, and a sign of that unity and peace and love which He so much desired amongst them, He gave them that which we are wont to call "The Sacrament of Love," the Blessed Eucharist. "All of you, take this and eat," He said, "it is my Body. And drink this, it is my Blood." Each and every one was to become united with Him in a sacramental union, a life-giving union, a union even closer than that which comes into being between a man and the food which nourishes him. And so, all being one with Him, they would be one with each other.

This He went on to explain in His beautiful teaching about the vine and the branches. There is, between a vine and the branches which draw life from it, the most perfect and intimate union. All the branches have the same life, the one life which is that of the vine. So it was to be with them. "He who eats me will live by me," He had said on a previous occasion. Now they had eaten Him; they were one with Him, living by Him, all sharing one life together. "I have bestowed my love upon you," He went on, "just as my Father has bestowed His love upon me. Live on, then, in my love. This is my commandment, that you should love one another as I have loved you."

And finally, in what is known as the great High-priestly prayer which our Lord prayed to His Father after this first Mass, He pleaded again and again that His followers might be truly one. "I pray for those entrusted to me," He said, "and not only for them, but for those who are to find faith in me through their word; that they may all be one . . . And I have given them the privilege that they should all be one, as we are one; that while thou art in me, I may be in them, and so they may be perfectly made one."

That, my dear brethren, is the foundation and cause of our unity; by the Holy Eucharist Christ is in us, and so we may be perfectly made one with each other. Our Lord gave us the Eucharist to unify us, to build us up into His Mystical Body, incorporated into that perfect unity which belongs to a living organism. As an early martyr succinctly expressed it: "The Church makes the Eucharist, and the Eucharist makes the Church." It is, in fact, by means of the Eucharist that all the members of the Church are unified. "The special grace of this sacrament," says St. Thomas Aquinas, "is the unity of the Mystical Body, the Church, which this sacrament both signifies and causes." And we find that statement echoed in the Secret of the Mass for the Feast of the Eucharist, Corpus Christi: "Grant to Thy Church, O Lord, the gifts of unity and peace which are mystically signified by these offerings."

From the circumstances in which Christ gave us the Mass we see, then, that it is a sacrifice of fraternal unity. And the same appears from the circumstances in which the Church bids us to celebrate it tonight.

On this day there are no private Masses; each Christian community is to come together at one time as one body; even though there may be several priest-members, there is but one Mass on one altar; a single sacrifice in which all, whether priests or laity, are to share. All, including the priests, are to receive Communion at the hands of the one who presides at the altar of this one sacrifice so that all may be united in the one sacred meal.

This was the invariable practice of the early Church for many centuries, not merely on special occasions but as the normal thing. Every Christian, whether priest or layman, came every Sunday to the one Mass celebrated by the bishop or the priest appointed by him to preside. Even when the increase and spread of the population made it necessary to multiply Mass centres with priests as celebrants, it was made clear that these were but extensions or multilocations of the one bishop's Mass; for the bishop sent a part of his own Eucharist to each priest celebrating as his representative, that it might be dropped into the priest's chalice. In recent centuries it has become impossible to continue the practice of having only one Mass in each church so that all the congregation may assemble together on one occasion. This is, however, the ideal; and as such it is preserved for us on Holy Thursday as a reminder of this fundamental aspect of the Mass as the sacrifice of unity. When, however, the number of communicants demands it, provision is made in the new legislation for one or the other low Mass before or after the solemn Last Supper celebration.

In early days, too, the unity of all was shown by the fact that at any Mass there was distributed to the faithful only the Sacred Bread which had then and there been consecrated in the very Mass they were offering. One loaf or one batch of loaves was consecrated and broken up amongst them; they were not given the Eucharist consecrated at some previous Mass: it was of *this same Mass* that they received their share in the banquet. Though now-a-days reasons of convenience have led to the practice of giving Communion from a ciborium consecrated at some previous Mass and reserved in the tabernacle, we are reminded by the Pope in his encyclical *Mediator Dei* that the old way of doing it is still the ideal. He wishes it to be done even now whenever it is possible. And, on the occasion of reforming the Holy Week services, he has made the ideal compulsory for this one occasion in the year—the "Mass of the Lord's Supper." For it is prescribed that the tabernacle is to be empty before the Mass begins, and that the hosts distributed in Communion are to be consecrated at this same Mass, in order that all may share in one and the same sacred meal.

The idea behind the regulation is that expressed by St. Paul to the Corinthians: "Is not the bread we break a participation in Christ's Body? The one bread makes us one body, though we are many in number; the same bread is shared by all." Moreover, as the Pope reminds us, if those who are present receive particles consecrated at the same Mass, "real fulfilment is given to the words of the Canon: 'that as many of us as have received the body and blood of Thy Son by partaking of this altar, may be filled with every heavenly blessing and grace.'"

Of all the blessings and graces we may receive this evening it is clear, then, that the grace which the Church most desires us to draw from this Mass is the grace of fraternal charity. We are to renew our determination to show our love for Christ by observing His favorite commandment—that we have love for one another. So, as we become united with Him in our Holy Thursday Communion we should ask Him with all the fervour which our memory of the Last Supper can inspire, that He will grant to us "those blessings of peace and unity which are mystically signified by our offerings."

GOOD FRIDAY

*Behold the wood of the Cross, on which hung
the Saviour of the world! Come, let us adore.*
—(Invitation to the Veneration of the Cross).

The cruelty of fallen man has invented many ways of
putting to death those who have been judged by their fellows
to be criminals. History relates that men have been hanged,
disembowelled, torn asunder, broken on wheels, boiled in oil,
buried alive; but it is generally agreed that no form of execu-
tion has ever been more horrible or more shameful than
crucifixion. We have listened, surely with pity and contrition,
to the story of how our Lord underwent this ghastly torture
for our sakes; we have solemnly prayed that He, who was
mercy incarnate, would grant the fruits of His passion and
cross to all those who stand in need of mercy. And now we
come to the climax of the Good Friday liturgy, the Veneration of the Cross.

But if the Cross is such a shameful thing, how has it come
about that we treat it with such honor? The reason is that
we are followers of Christ, the great Conqueror. It was by
the Cross that He conquered; we look beyond His death to
the victory He thereby gained; we look through the shame
heaped upon Him by man to the glory conferred upon Him

by God His Father. To those without faith the Cross is, indeed, a scandal; but "it is for us," as St. Paul said, "to glory in the Cross of our Lord Jesus Christ in whom is our salvation; through whom we have been saved and set free."

The early Christians loved the Cross; but living, as they did, under persecution in the Roman world which viewed the Cross as nothing but a gibbet of shame, they could not express their veneration openly. They had neither crucifixes nor pictures of the crucifixion, and could do no more than indicate their devotion by using symbols of which they alone knew the meaning.

But when the Emperor Constantine was converted in the fourth century and gave freedom to the Church, all that was soon changed. Before long the Cross became the most loved object of Christian artists and sculptors, and has ever since been held in the highest honor. Full of meaning, it stands above every altar and is embroidered on the vestments of priests. From reflecting walls and transparent windows of churches it reminds us of Christ's love; from towers and steeples it recalls to us His victory; it glints on the breasts of bishops and in the crowns of kings; as a silent preacher it stands in market places and by country roads. The Cross has inspired countless preachers and poets and writers and artists; for love of the Cross princes have renounced thrones, men have given up riches, women have veiled their beauty; missionaries have journeyed to remote lands to plant the Cross there, and martyrs have died to maintain it. And today, two thousand years after the Cross was erected on Calvary, its glory still shines forth among men.

The ceremony we are about to perform is very old. It began in Jerusalem, not long after the Empress Helena had discovered the relics of the True Cross. On Good Friday these relics were brought forth, and the bishop and all the faithful filed past to kiss the Cross in token of their love for Him who died upon it. The custom gradually spread to Rome, and thence throughout the whole Catholic world, a crucifix being used instead of a relic—for the True Cross cannot be everywhere.

And so now the Cross will be lifted up, not in a place of shame outside the gates of the old Jerusalem, but in a place of honor within the sanctuary of the new Jerusalem, the Church. It will be greeted, not by the mocking of scribes and pharisees and the blasphemies of pagans, but by the reverence and love of Christian people. The celebrant will unveil the crucifix little by little, each time singing to us an invitation: *"Ecce lignum crucis,* "Behold the wood of the Cross on which hung the Saviour of the world!" And we will manifest our devotion by sinking to our knees as we answer *"Venite adoremus,* Come, let us worship!" And after the clergy and altar servers have kissed the Cross, we shall, each in turn, come forward to kiss the sacred symbol.

And what, exactly, will our act of veneration mean? It should express outwardly what we feel, or ought to feel, inwardly. It is something like a sacramental act in that it is an outward sign of an inward reality. What matters above all is this inward reality; for merely kissing the Cross will not bring us grace unless we do it in the spirit of love and contrition. But if we approach with the dispositions that the Church hopes will be ours as the result of the Scripture readings and prayers which have gone before, directing to Him who was crucified for us the sign of love and honor which we pay to His image, then we will receive a blessing, a grace, an impulse to follow Him more closely and unite ourselves with Him.

Our Holy Father the Pope has recently decreed a most welcome change in today's liturgy. He has rendered it possible for you all now actually to unite yourselves sacramentally with the Victim of the Cross. For many centuries the Good

Friday service ended with this veneration of the Cross. Then came a period when the faithful were allowed, as it were unofficially, to receive Holy Communion even though the clergy were still bound by the official regulation of abstaining from the Eucharist. Later still, however, the clergy also were granted the same privilege, so that everyone could receive Holy Communion on Good Friday. But as time went on there came a sad diminution in the frequency of Communion by the people; they ceased altogether to receive on Good Friday and the only one who continued to do so was the officiating priest. Thus things remained for a very long time, and became stabilized by law. So that when frequent Communion was restored by St. Pius X and happily gained ground among the faithful, it was natural that they should desire to receive their Saviour on the day when they contemplated the death whereby He had saved them. But alas, as the law stood, they were not allowed to do so.

You should, therefore, be very grateful to our present Holy Father for changing that law and permitting you today to receive Holy Communion with the priest. It is to be hoped that very many, in fact all of you, will do so. Our Lord has told us: "If any man will be my disciple, let him take up his cross and follow Me." And this, of course, does not mean lifting up a material object and carrying it along; it means becoming like Christ as He was on His Cross, giving ourselves to God no matter what it may cost us; it means becoming victims with Christ, filled with the same spirit of obedience and devotion, inspired by faith and hope and love and gratitude. That is what we should strive for today; and nothing is better calculated to arouse these dispositions in us than sacramental union with the very Victim Who offered Himself for us upon the Cross.

"We adore Thee, O Christ, and we bless Thee, because by Thy Holy Cross Thou hast redeemed the world."

For Lent and Easter...

THE WAY OF THE CROSS

An arrangement consisting of texts culled from Biblical and Liturgical sources. The *Stabat Mater,* in English, is given between Stations. Edited for parish use. Illustrated.

HOLY WEEK AND EASTER

A full-length liturgical commentary on the liturgy of Holy Week *and* the Easter octave by Rev. Jean Gaillard, O.S.B. Completely revised and substantially enlarged according to the spirit and legislation of the Restored Holy Week Liturgy.

Of special excellence is the author's use of Scriptural texts in the light of patristic and liturgical tradition. After introductory chapters on the nature of the Paschal mystery and the spirit of the feasts, we find a liturgical commentary on the days of Holy Week, with a continuation on the octave of special graces, *The Week of the White Robes.* 180 pages.

THE MASSES OF HOLY WEEK AND EASTER VIGIL

Complete text of the Holy Week Masses, arranged for congregational participation. Needed commentary included in context. Edited by Fr. Godfrey Diekmann, O.S.B., editor of *Worship.* 190 pages.

EASTER TO PENTECOST FAMILY CUSTOMS

How to carry the profound meaning of Easter's liturgy into the daily acts of family life. By Helen McLoughlin.

Partial list of chapter topics:

Easter Night Home Service	In the Kitchen
Easter Water and Blessings	Rogation Days
The Easter Lamb	The Cenacle in the Home
Cards for Grace at Meals	Gingerbread for Whitsun
Music and Song	Monday

ELEGANTLY ILLUSTRATED IN COLORED PICTURES

Send for complete listings

LITURGICAL PRESS   Collegeville, Minn.